401K Rescue

WHY YOUR EMPLOYEES HATE YOUR 401K
AND HOW TO FIX IT LIKE A FIDUCIARY

J.D. Kaiser, MBA
Accredited Investment Fiduciary®
with cartoons by Pulitzer-Prize Winner Steve Breen

401k Rescue Experts
SEATTLE, WASHINGTON

Copyright © 2019 by J.D. Kaiser.

All rights reserved. No part of this publication may be reproduced, distributed or transmitted in any form or by any means, including photocopying, recording, or other electronic or mechanical methods, without the prior written permission of the publisher, except in the case of brief quotations embodied in critical reviews and certain other noncommercial uses permitted by copyright law. For permission requests, write to the publisher at the address below.

All website references and citations current as of October 2019.

J.D. Kaiser/401k Rescue Experts.
6023 Roosevelt Way NE
Seattle, Washington/98115
info@401kRescueExperts.com

Book layout ©2013 BookDesignTemplates.com
Cartoons by Steve Breen

401K Rescue / J.D. Kaiser. —1st ed.
ISBN 9781700306258

Contents

Make Yourself the 401(k) Advocate for Your Company i
How Jennifer Went from 401(k) Distress to Success vii
    What's in It for You? viii

Chapter One: Why Small Business Owners Need to Avoid 401(k) Mistakes 1
    This Story Could Have Ended in Disaster 1
    Why Small Business Owners Want 401(k) Plans 3
    Are You Ready for an Audit? 9

Chapter Two: Behold, the Four Biggest 401(k) Mistakes 13
    The Four Common Mistakes 15
    Why Your Employees Hate Their 401(k) 22

Chapter Three: Overcoming 401(k) Mistakes in Four Easy Steps 29
    What Do You Do Next? 31
    Employers Want Their Employees to Have Great Education on Investing and Retirement 37
    A Personal Fiduciary Advisor Makes the Team Stronger 39
    Summary 42

Chapter Four: Let the IPS Be Your GPS 43
    An IPS Is Not Required But It Is a "Best Practice" 43
    7 Aspects of an Investment Policy Statement 44
    Taking the Census of America's 401(k) Plans 53

Chapter Five: Create an All-Star Lineup of Investments 55
    How to Select Twenty from a Field of Thousands 56

When an Employee Cannot Decide 58

Summary 59

Chapter Six: If You Think Education Is Costly, You're Going to Hate Ignorance 61

Great Education Increases Participation 61

A True Fiduciary Advisor's Goals Are Aligned with the Participant's Goals 62

During the '08 Recession, Employees Cried Out for Guidance 64

Open Communication with Employees Is Key 66

Summary 67

Chapter Seven: How's Your Retirement Financial Knowledge? 69

Pop Quiz 69

Summary 72

Chapter Eight: Three Rs of Retirement Plans: Rules, Risk, and Expert Relief 73

Wait, What If the Rules Change? 74

Might I Get Sued? Prepare, Don't Panic 77

Hire an Expert—You'll be Glad You Did 80

Summary 82

Chapter Nine: An Invisible Army Is Behind Each Independent Advisor 83

Summary 95

Chapter Ten: Doing an RFP— Be Careful What You Ask For ... 97

How to Save Yourself Time and Trouble 98

Is It Time to Get Competitive Bids? 104

Summary 105

Chapter Eleven: How Two Companies Switched Advisors 107
    Pacific Rehabilitation Centers 107
    A 300-Employee Nonprofit 112
    Summary 117
Chapter Twelve: Closing the Deal in Choosing an Expert 119
    The Day Mom Shattered My Business Plan 119
    Don't Get Mad, Get a Fiduciary 125
About the Author 131
Twenty Terms Every Plan Sponsor Must Know 133
Accredited Investment Fiduciary® Standards 137

Dedicated to all those 401(k) participants, plan sponsors, and business owners who are wading through confusion and difficulty with their plans. Don't give up—help is on the way!

Executive Summary

If you only read one page of this book, it should be this page!

The basic equation:

- A 401(k) Plan Sponsor is required by the U.S. Department of Labor to be a fiduciary.
- A fiduciary is required to act solely in the best interest of the 401(k) plan participants.
- The Plan Sponsor is personally liable for compliance and regulatory violations.
- If you are not an expert in all phases of 401(k) plan management, you must hire and monitor an expert.
- This book won't make you an expert, but it will provide you with the tools to choose and monitor your own 401(k) expert.

If you only have time to do one thing, check the fees in your 401k.

Every investment has a fee. To use a bottle of water as analogy for your investments…If you were buying the exact same bottle of water, would you buy it at a movie theater ($5), a convenience store ($2.49), or Costco (25 cents)? To get the best value for your money you would go to Costco, wouldn't you? Why would you pay $5 for the same bottle of water that you could get at 25 cents? Do you know if your 401k investments are bought from a movie theater, convenience store, or Costco?

As the 401(k) Plan Sponsor you must act in the best interest of your participants by paying the lowest possible fee available.

To determine if you are in compliance with U.S. Department of Labor regulations (fiduciary duties), you should get a benchmark report with fee analysis www.401k-Benchmark.com.

WHAT YOU CAN GET OUT OF THIS BOOK

Make Yourself the 401(k) Hero for Your Company

J.D. Kaiser here. Let me tell you my story. Then, I want to hear yours.

I've helped people with their money for more than twenty-five years. In the beginning, I was helping folks my parents' age protect their homes and money from being taken from nursing home spend-downs. This was a very frugal crowd of folks who grew up during the depression. I was helping people like my Mom.

I filled hotel rooms (no free coffee and no bathroom breaks) and educated everyone who came about the basics of asset protection. Enough of these folks became my clients that my business grew to have two offices and staff.

This was a very popular service. I used to tell my young daughter (twenty years ago now) that in every neighborhood in Seattle, I could find a client or two who'd be glad to invite us in for a cup of coffee. My daughter reminded me she didn't like coffee and asked if they'd have some milk and cookies, instead.

My daughter and me back in the day.

I started taking Polaroid pictures of these people and put the pictures on the wall. The following picture shows just one corner of my office.

Here's a closeup. You can see Barney and Margaret Welch. He was a fire captain and grew great flowers, too!

I loved it. Coming into work each day, I was—and still am—greeted by the faces of people I helped. To this day, the corner of Polaroid pictures reminds me we each have our own story. We each have hopes and dreams and fears, and it was my job to do my best for them.

Those who are still living are now in their eighties and nineties. I like to call them "Ladies in Their Eighties" (the men don't care what I call them!).

Time went on. One Christmas I wanted to have a get-together for all these nice people. I sent out invitations and got a call from one of the ladies. She said, "I'd like to go but I don't drive at night."

Duh! What was I thinking? I quickly regrouped and sent out a van to pick them all up and take them home. What a nice night it was!

"Ladies in Their Eighties" night on the town.

Then the baby boomers started to think about retirement.

I figured the best way to help this group was to develop and teach a retirement class. It was not a free dinner deal, though. It was a real class that spanned more than three sessions of two hours each. Each student paid a tuition. I even gave tests.

You know what the biggest complaint was? They wanted more time. I tried to pack a lot of information into those classes and might have gone a little overboard.

It was so popular that I was working nights and Saturdays just to keep up. Everyone who attended the class got a solid education. And enough of these students went on to become my clients; they were still hungry for more knowledge, and I kept very busy.

At every class, we discussed 401(k) programs. I had students bring in their statements. We went online. We looked at investments. We tried to judge performance against an index, get dividend information, and everything else I was teaching.

Then, I gave the students some homework. Call your 401(k)'s toll-free number and ask them if you can roll your money over to an IRA. (This is called an in-service distribution.) Half of the students who made the call told me that the rep on the other end of the line didn't even know what they were talking about! (You might have the same experience just trying to get information. Frustrating, isn't it?)

I was *shocked* at the level of frustration my students had with their 401(k)s.

I really didn't expect this at all.

Fast forward a few years. I decided to learn everything I could about managing a 401(k). Seems logical right?

As an educated person, financial advisor, and fiduciary, I assumed there would be plenty of material out there to teach me what I wanted to learn, right?

Wrong!

You'd be surprised at how difficult it is to find solid information to help guide a financial advisor who wants to manage 401(k) programs.

Being perseverant (okay, some might call me obsessed), I dug deep, and now I'm that expert.

I've got a Master of Business Administration degree, I'm a fiduciary, and I have specialized training that earned me the credential of Accredited Investment Fiduciary. I've also got years of experience teaching difficult financial topics in plain English.

So, let me sum it up.

What's in it for me? This is really important.

When I help one person I feel great. It's not just a job, I'm really helping someone.

When I teach a class and help many people, I feel that much better. I know I'm affecting them for the better for the rest of their life.

And now, when I help all the employees covered under a 401(k), I feel fantastic. I'm helping a ton of people all at once to have a better life.

I think I was put on this earth to help everyday people understand some very difficult and confusing topics, like money.

Now what about you?

What's in it for you?

I want to make you the champion!

I want to make you the hero to your family, and the ally to all the employees in your company. You might have a little or a lot of experience with 401(k)s. I will give you the tools to make that 401(k) the best it can be.

And if you get stuck, or need help, I'm just a call away. You can call me at 206-362-0503. I'll be glad to help you. And hopefully I can put your picture on my wall!

~ J.D. Kaiser, September 2019

INTRODUCTION

How Jennifer Went from 401(k) Distress to Success

Let me tell you a story about Jennifer K.

Jennifer is a responsible business owner. Jennifer (real story, but name and some details changed to protect confidentiality) had worked hard for twenty years to grow her physical therapy business. Jennifer chose physical therapy as a career because she wanted to help patients to function without back, neck, and other pain. The business had survived its own growing pains, from the start-up days to the recession of 2008.

One day Jennifer decided her business was at a crossroads.

"To protect my own retirement and keep good employees, I want to start a 401(k)-retirement plan for the company," she told her company insurance agent.

So, she decided to pursue setting up a 401(k) plan. Being a busy business owner, Jennifer did not have time to do tons and tons of research, so she tried to do it the simple way with a group variable annuity from her big brand-name insurance company.

However, this created a conflict. Jennifer learned that not all 401(k) plans are created equal. While it was the simple approach, Jennifer soon learned that simple is not always good enough.

Employees complained about the amount of fees associated with the plan. Those employees were right, but that was not the worst of it. With a heavy heart, I had to inform Jennifer that she made four classic mistakes.

"Sorry, Jennifer, your plan has no investment policy, no all-star investment options, no way to monitor investment performance, and no investment education component," I informed her. "On top of that, as the plan sponsor, if things go wrong, you are 100 percent liable."

Jennifer's 401(k) dream had the potential to be a nightmare. Jennifer worked with me to follow the four steps to do the 401(k) right. Together we created a plan with a written investment policy, we gave the employees (and Jennifer) a variety of solid investment options, we made sure investment performance was monitored, and we provided her employees with valuable investment education.

"Now I can look my employees in the eye (and myself in the mirror) knowing we are winning the 401(k) game, not losing it," said Jennifer. "The changes we made allow us to focus time and energy on providing what really matters, helping our physical therapy patients restore bodily function and reduce pain."

What's in It for You?

Whether you are a business owner, human resources (HR) manager, or are responsible for your company's 401(k), you can learn a valuable lesson from Jennifer's story. This book is a guide for how to prosper from a 401(k) and how to avoid the pitfalls. I am optimistic about what a 401(k) program can do for a business, it's owner, and the employees. But only if they avoid the biggest drawbacks.

My hope is this book will help you make your 401(k) the best it can be and be the advocate for all those counting on you.

DO YOU UNDERSTAND YOUR FIDUCIARY RESPONSIBILITIES?

Once your company establishes your 401(k) plan, you have to name a Plan Sponsor. The Plan Sponsor is an individual required by the Department of Labor to act as a fiduciary.

As a fiduciary you must:

- Act solely in the interest of plan participants.
    - Every decision that you make has to be in the <u>best interest</u> of the participants.
- Exercise prudent judgement.
    - Would a third-party expert reviewing your work consider your decisions to be sound?
- Follow ERISA compliant plan documents.
    - Will your Plan pass a Department of Labor audit?
- Offer highly rated and diversified investments.
    - Your choices must be suitable for a wide variety of risk levels and be scored highly by the latest FinTech analysis software.
- Pay only reasonable plan expenses
    - Don't pay more than you have to. You insure this by "benchmarking" your Plan

What does this mean to you?

1. If you are the Plan Sponsor, you have to be an expert to carry out these Department of Labor requirements.
2. If you're not an expert, then you should make the prudent decision to hire an expert.
3. This book gives you the basics on what to look for when hiring the right expert.

CHAPTER ONE

Why Small Business Owners Need to Avoid 401(k) Mistakes

This is a cautionary tale about what can happen at a small business that makes mistakes with its 401(k) plan.

Employee lawsuits used to be the problem of just the mega-plans, but not anymore. Fortunately, this story has a happy ending.

This Story Could Have Ended in Disaster

The year was 2016 and the place was a nine-location family-owned repair business in the Midwest with one-hundred employees. Let's call the president Kevin (the name and some details have changed, of course). Kevin's family, who founded the business in 1976, cared about the workers and wanted to be competitive by offering a 401(k) for employees.

Kevin's repair business went into crisis mode when some employees filed a class-action lawsuit, which echoed similar allegations that have been brought against sponsors of big business 401(k) plans. Specifically, the suit alleged that Kevin and the chief financial officer of the business failed to engage "in a prudent process to evaluate service providers and assess reasonableness of fees" for handling the company's $9 million-plus 401(k) profit-sharing plan.

Kevin wanted to pursue a successful resolution to the employees' various concerns.

The conflict was over fees, and fees matter when it comes to a 401(k). For an in depth look at fees, you can visit: https://www.dol.gov/sites/dolgov/files/EBSA/about-ebsa/our-activities/resource-center/publications/a-look-at-401k-plan-fees.pdf

Is Your 401(k) Plan Set Up in the Best Interest of Your Employees?

As the plan sponsor, a business owner like Kevin must make financial decisions that are in the best interest of the employee participants. Kevin and the business came to understand that the United States Supreme Court itself has found that a *"prudent 401(k) selection and management process"* is a legal requirement for plan sponsors. According to Justice Stephen Breyer, plan fiduciaries face a *"continuing duty to review investments that includes a duty to remove imprudent investments."*

Kevin breathed a sigh of relief when the case against his company was voluntarily withdrawn.

However, the aftermath is not so great for other small business owners. Gretchen Russell, a lawyer and Employee Retirement Income Security Act (ERISA) researcher for the firm Pension Consultants, said the suit "tolls the end of what seemed to be small to mid-sized plans' former exemption for lawsuits."[1]

---

[1] Nick Thornton. BenefitsPro.com. July 7, 2016. "Case Against Small Plan Sponsor Voluntarily Withdrawn."
https://www.benefitspro.com/2016/07/07/case-against-small-plan-sponsor-voluntarily-withdr/?slreturn=20190010231143.

Why Small Business Owners Want 401(k) Plans

Small business owners should set up 401(k) plans for two major reasons.

Obviously, the first is to help their own retirement. The second reason is to help their businesses.

That's because every small business owner wants to find and keep the best employees they can. Satisfied employees keep customers satisfied, and satisfied customers are one key to a sustainable business.

So, what do good employees want? Evidence shows the best and brightest employees want financial education and sound investment advice.

They are giving their all for the company and they want to know the company has their financial back.

Some employees are jaded, too, and not engaged with plans they consider poorly designed or run.

The opportunity: At large corporations, a 401(k) is a standard employee benefit. According to a 2015 Retirement Plan Sponsor Sentiment Survey, conducted by TD Ameritrade, a 401(k) is the most requested benefit after health care. According to the United States Government Accountability Office, only 14 percent of small businesses offer a 401(k).

This retirement savings vehicle is a great deal for the employer because they can defer a lot of money. By allowing employees to defer money, the owner, who draws much more money during profitable times than the rank-and-file employee, can defer a substantially greater amount. That's fair—retirement lifestyle expectations are built on working career incomes.

It is a competitive advantage to be a place where good talent wants to work because you have a plan.

Business Is Great—Until It's Time to Retire

We probably all know an entrepreneur who chased his or her dream. If the business model was sound, if the economy was conducive—two big ifs to be sure—that person may be prospering today, taking frequent mini-vacations or Wednesday golf outings by leaving the shop to a trusted employee in one of the jobs this entrepreneur created.

It wasn't always so. When asked about the early days, these entrepreneurs will tell you they scraped together as much capital as possible. They opened with an idea, a drive and a prayer. The first years were filled with 14-hour days because they couldn't afford help.

The plan was for the spouse to stay at home with the kids or just put in eight-hour shifts at that secure corporate job. Forget the plan. Inevitably the spouse gets drawn into the business, doing errands, bookkeeping, or mom-to-the-rescue.

Kerry Hannon, in Forbes article, tells the story of her father.

"My dad was a small business owner whose engineering and consulting firm provided a solid income for him and supported our family. When he realized none of his four children were going to take over the business, he sold it at age 70. Dad didn't have a retirement savings plan per se—the sale of the business was his retirement plan (plus Social Security and some rental income)."

Hannon quotes David Deeds, a University of St. Thomas in Minneapolis professor: "The business is their retirement plan. The plan is that when they retire, they are either going to transfer the business to a family member in exchange for a share of future wealth or a buyout, or they are going to sell it off and turn that into cash."[2]

---

[2] Kerry Hannon, Forbes, 5 Retirement Planning Tips for Small Business Owners. Dec. 8, 2016.

The owners have fallen into a trap of continuing to pour money into the business, but not into their retirement savings. The transition from struggling start-up to success may have sneaked up on them.

The risks are many. Small farming hamlets across America's midlands have withered in part because none of the kids wanted to stay on the farm and ignore the siren call of the city. Health issues can crop up without warning and if the entrepreneur is really the heart of the business, an emergency sale may bring a depressingly low price. Or, the economy changes. The days of a service station on every corner are gone and with them the opportunities for a multitude of mechanics to become franchise owners. Storefronts renting DVDs were a lucrative niche—for a while. Now, even Blockbuster is busted. Can a TV repairman charge what he should today without fear of the customer simply walking out and buying a new set?

Entrepreneurs who are young and energetic enough can always get training and start over with a new idea. Those with gray hair, a touch of arthritis, and adorable grandchildren had better hope they have an adequate retirement plan and savings.

You may have something, but is it enough?

That's where a financial advisor specialist or consultant can make a difference. Just as a physical health exam is a good idea, so is a financial checkup by an experienced advisor who can provide a fresh set of eyes.

Some small business owners reason that a 401(k) plan is an unnecessary extra expense. They feel that a 401(k) is a luxury that a small business can do without.

---

https://www.forbes.com/sites/nextavenue/2016/12/08/5-retirement-planning-tips-for-small-business-owners/#2bdb0e1b28ce

That thinking is a gross miscalculation. Here is why: Not having a plan makes you seem like a poor option as a place to work. If it comes down to choosing job A or B, the employer of choice is one that offers a 401(k) plan. Potential employees reason: "If they can't get a 401(k) done, what other challenges are they hiding?"

Here are the hard dollars and sense of a 401(k) plan: these plans are a recruiting magnet.

Times Are Changing—Pensions vs. 401(k)s

In the past, employees were guaranteed at least a certain amount of income through traditional pension plans offered by employers. These days, pension plans are becoming rare.

These are also called defined-benefit plans. Traditional pensions put the risk on the employer. Employees were promised so much per year of service and the employer had to set aside funds to meet the projected payments. If investments fared poorly or the industry went through exceedingly tough times, the employer was still on the hook.

Along came the 401(k) plans, named after a provision in the tax code, which shifted the burden of risk to the employee. These are also known as defined-contribution plans, as the employer's responsibility is limited to offering and administering the plan and possibly matching a portion of the employee's contribution. If a company does away with traditional pensions but does not offer a 401(k) vehicle, employees have lost the benefit of having any company assistance whatsoever in preparing for retirement.

So, potential workers are quick to realize the benefits of joining a company that offers a 401(k) plan. If a person has the choice between two equally appealing job offers and one company offers a 401(k) plan, it's likely to sway his or her decision. In other words, 401(k) plans are a must-have benefit that will help attract top talent to your small business.

An easy way to make your company's plan the best possible magnet, suggests the staff of Insperity.com, is to talk to your current employees. In a blog post from February 11, 2011, titled "5 Common Problems with Small Business Retirement Plans," they recommend, "Find out what factors would entice them to participate in the company's plan. Ask them what they think would be a reasonable contribution rate. Also, consider researching what types of plans other businesses in your industry are offering."[3]

A Great 401(k) Shows You Care—And It's Good for Business

401(k) plans help reduce employee turnover. Nearly 40 percent of small-business employees say they would leave their current job for one that provides a 401(k), Plan Adviser magazine reports.[4] Further, retirement plans are among one of the top ten reasons why employees chose their employer, according to a recent American Association of Retired Persons (AARP) survey.[5]

Offering a 401(k) plan not only shows you care about your employees, but also helps you be more competitive in the marketplace. Retaining employees means you'll spend less money on recruiting and training new ones.

Employee turnover can be staggering, hitting 47 percent annually for retail employees in California, according to a 2015 survey cited by Ahmad El-Najjar in "The Higher Cost of Hiring:

---

[3] Staff. Insperity.com. February 11, 2011. "5 Common Problems with Small Business Retirement Plans."
https://www.insperity.com/blog/5-common-problems-with-small-business-retirement-plans/#

[4] Lee Barney. Plan Adviser. August 15, 2017. "Majority of Small Businesses Do Not Offer Retirement Health Benefits."
https://www.planadviser.com/majority-of-small-businesses-do-not-offer-retirement-health-benefits/.

[5] David Walker. AARP. March 27, 2017. "Opinion: Let States Help People Retire."
www.AARP.org/retirement/Planning-for-retirement/info-2017/states-help-people-retire-FD.html.

Rethinking Employee Retention."[6] New York was even higher at nearly 56 percent. The statistics are compiled by the United States Bureau of Labor Statistics' Job Openings and Labor Turnover Program. Besides being a magnet for hiring quality employees, 401(k) plans that promote employee retention can reduce expensive training costs. For a retail employee earning $10 hour an hour in 2012, the Center for American Progress found, the cost of hiring and training averaged $3,328 per worker.

401(k) plans help save on small-business taxes. A business might be eligible for a special $500 tax credit for the first three years of its 401(k) plan. If the $500 tax credit for starting up a 401(k) plan isn't convincing enough, then the tax deductions for employer contributions should be.

As an additional bonus, an owner, by investing in his or her own plan, can save on personal taxes, too.

Business Owners Can Sock Away a Lot of Money —And Reduce Their Taxes

In his white paper titled "Challenges Facing Privately Held Businesses," consultant Derrick Handwerk points out that entrepreneurs can combine 401(k) plans and traditional pensions to put away a lot of money.[7]

How much?

According to Julius Smetona of DeSales Associates, a fifty-year-old can contribute a total of $354,654 in 2018. The immediate tax savings potential is enormous.

401(k) plans help small-business owners support their own retirements. Too many small-business owners focus solely on the

---

[6] Ahmad El-Najjar. Townsquared. March 4, 2016. "The Higher Cost of Hiring: Rethinking Employee Retention."
https://townsquared.com/ts/resources/employee-retention/.

[7] Derrick Handwerk. October 2016. "Challenges Facing Privately Held Businesses." http://www.handwerkmfo.com/p/white-paper.

success of their businesses while shortchanging their own personal retirement security. A 401(k) plan makes sense regardless of how long you've been in business. Even if you decide to start up another company, you can simply roll over your 401(k) balance to a new account.

The temptation for sole proprietors is to pump cash flow back into the business. Yet, diverting money toward their own retirement through these tax-sheltered retirement plans defers taxes until withdrawal years later. There are fairness rules—contribution matches and eligibility must be extended to all employees, not just top executives—but management figures with high responsibility and high compensation will have the most discretionary income and ability to participate fully.

Small business owners should set up 401(k) retirement plans. And they need to do it by avoiding the four biggest mistakes, which are the focus of the next chapter.

Are You Ready for an Audit?

You should understand that your 401(k) plan could be audited by the Department of Labor. If you don't pass, they very well could bring in the Internal Revenue Service.

The IRS Has Found a Mistake. Now What?

Who better to know the most common 401(k) plan mistakes companies make than the Internal Revenue Service?

Who better to explain what was done wrong and how to fix it than the IRS?

Um, one out of two isn't bad.

Well, to be fair, the IRS website does try to provide information in plain English. It's just that acronyms and code section citations tend to get in the way.

The common mistakes can be found on the IRS website by searching for "IRS," "401(k)" and "common mistakes." Or, you can look at www.irs.gov/retirement-plans/401k-plan-fix-it-guide.

To err is to be human, and mistakes will happen.

The IRS Fix-it Guide lists twelve common mistakes, how to find the mistake, how to fix the mistake, and how to avoid the mistake. Following are the all-too-common twelve.

- You haven't updated your plan document within the past few years to reflect recent law changes.
- You didn't base the plan operations on the terms of the plan document. Failure to follow plan terms is a very common mistake.
- You didn't use the plan definition of compensation correctly for all deferrals and allocations.
- Employer matching contributions weren't made to all appropriate employees.
- The plan failed 401(k) Actual Deferral Percentage (ADP) and Actual Contribution Percentage (ACP) nondiscrimination tests.
- Eligible employees weren't given the opportunity to make an elective deferral (exclusion of eligible employees.)
- Elective deferrals weren't limited to the IRC Section 402(g) amounts for the year and excess deferrals weren't distributed.
- You haven't timely deposited employee elective deferrals.
- Participant loans don't conform to the requirements of IRC Section 72(p) or are prohibited under IRC Section 4975.
- Hardship distributions weren't made properly.
- The plan was top heavy, and the required minimum contributions weren't made to the plan.
- You haven't filed a Form 5500-series return this year.

So far, so good? Surely everyone in HR is up to speed on ADP and ACP nondiscrimination tests or the prohibitions of IRC Section 4975, right?

Failure to update plan documents is a serious matter. How can you follow the rules if you don't know what the current rules are? The IRS explanation of finding, fixing, and avoiding mistakes fills twelve pages. When tax laws change, you must amend your written plan.

The IRS advises that to show you have made timely amendments you should review a sheaf of documents including the original plan document, all subsequent amendments or restatements, adoption agreements, any IRS opinion or advisory letter, any IRS discrimination letter, and board of directors' resolutions and minutes.

Let's take something simpler, an example of a computation mistake. Your company matches half of employee contributions up to 6 percent. So, if the employee contributes 6 percent, the company makes a matching contribution of 3 percent. The trouble is that in 2014, worker Carla made an 8 percent deferral. Instead of matching half of 6 percent, a new clerical employee only had the company match half of 3 percent.

Correcting the mistake only involves a review of old payroll records, a lot of computations and three pages of explanation on how to do it.

MORAL

You're running a business. If business is good, you're concentrating on hiring more employees, leasing additional space, and going after additional market share while the economy is booming. There's the new software installation that IT says is almost ready. Oh yes, does the computer system still have sufficient safeguards against being hacked?

How much time do you want to devote to training the staff on avoiding and fixing common mistakes on 401(k) plans? Or would you rather hire an independent financial advisor to handle the burden?

CHAPTER TWO

Behold, the Four Biggest 401(k) Mistakes

If you're new to managing a 401(k) or haven't reviewed your current plan, it makes sense to know the most common pitfalls you need to watch out for.

The wake-up call at smaller firms, say those with less than $100 million in assets in their retirement savings programs, tends to come from the company's human resources department.

Employees wander in with complaints. It's a trickle at first, then a growing stream.

"There are too few choices. Why don't we have target date retirement funds? Or a technology sector fund?"

Or, "There are so many options. I'm overwhelmed. How do I know what's right for me?"

Or, "Our funds haven't gained much at all the past two years. The (other) fund family has been growing across the board. Who chooses our funds, and can we get a different manager?"

Or, "The stock market has been plunging lately. I'm scared. Should I take my money out of stocks and put it into cash until the economy gets better?"

Or, "Does the company pay the fees for the plan or is it taken out of my contribution? How much are the fees, anyhow? Why doesn't anyone seem to know?"

Finally, you walk into the corner office. "Boss, the employees are upset about our 401(k) program because—well, for a variety of reasons. We have to do something."

"Gee, why are they unhappy? We offer a contribution match—free money—and half of those signed up don't even bother to participate enough to collect that. I don't know what to do. Have you called the people who set up the plan? What do they say?"

That's the wake-up call, though the danger signs were present, if unnoticed, even before. Employees were talking one-to-one but were not sure who in management to approach, or perhaps were too timid. New hires were declining to sign up or were setting aside way too little in automatic deductions to save for retirement.

Companies have gone to considerable effort and expense to set up retirement savings plans through painless payroll deduction.

Yet four common mistakes have allowed what should be a welcomed benefit to degrade into a source of frustration.

Before naming the four common mistakes, here's something you need to understand. The company is the plan sponsor. As a sponsor, the company can hire experts to do the heavy lifting or fiduciary role. It can shift much of the responsibility or legal liability to the experts. ***The plan sponsor (the company) is ultimately responsible.*** Therefore, if you are not an expert, you have the duty to seek out an expert.

In a future chapter, we'll explain how one becomes an expert. They may be subject to a fiduciary standard, they may be accredited by a recognized leader in the industry and may receive ongoing training for ethics and stay current on 401(k) best practices. This means they have training, credentials, and such and are qualified to offer investment advice to the employees if the sponsor (owner) so wishes. The fiduciaries have an obligation to put the employees first, ahead of their own remuneration.

Other "experts" may be representatives of insurance companies who are not eligible to offer investment advice. Or they may be representatives of stock brokerages who are paid with commissions on the products they sell. Do they have a conflict in whose best interest comes first? The standard they must meet is a lot lower. Regardless of the size of the commission, is the product suitable for the client?

The Four Common Mistakes

These are the four common plan mistakes and are often the reason why the guy on the loading dock or the worried secretary says, "the company's 401(k) plan stinks."

- No investment policy statement, or a poorly crafted one. Outside advisors rightly tell their clients that the 401(k) Best Practices dictate the use of a formal investment policy statement (IPS) setting forth the goals and procedures for selecting, monitoring and replacing investments. Once adopted, the IPS should be followed.

- Lack of, or poor options. Next comes an investment lineup: all the options for the participants to consider. They should have the chance to be diversified among asset classes, stocks, bonds, small cap, large cap, and target-date retirement funds. Whether done by outside experts or in-house, the individuals involved should follow a prudent process in making those different investment options available.
- Little or no financial education offered. Companies should choose to have education or guidance available on basic concepts, enough so that an employee is not hopelessly bewildered. They may or may not wish to hire a third-party expert to offer employees advice on how much to invest or which products to select from the menu. The company has been proactive in deciding to offer a 401(k). It's a shame not to help the workers with a modicum of education understand how to get the most out of what is offered.
- Failure to monitor. Just because you created an appropriate menu years ago, that does not mean those choices are still the best ones for participants today. Fiduciaries need to monitor performance against benchmarks. They also need to be aware of new and perhaps lower-fee mutual fund offerings and alternatives to regular mutual funds, such as exchange-traded funds (ETFs).

If the boss and HR are unfamiliar with these topics, they are not alone. Some businesses and large university sponsors have learned that just leaving it up to some big-name company to take care of everything by default may not be the prudent course. Quite possibly, leaving it to a megafirm may not lead to lower fees or higher rates of return, especially if their representatives are not credentialed fiduciaries.

So, the four key problem areas leading to mistakes are:
- The lack of an investment policy statement
- Poor investment options,
- Financial education for participants and sponsors,
- And monitoring plan performance.

Investment Policy Statement

An investment policy statement is like a GPS system. It gives your 401(k) plan directions and desired outcomes.

For additional perspective, we turned to a good friend, Sharon Pivirotto. She is the owner of Pivirotto Resource Group in Pittsburgh, Pennsylvania, a twenty-year veteran of the financial industry and writes the "401(k) Best Practice Blog." She trains specialists to advise retirement savings programs.

> "Take the investment policy statement," Sharon said. "It must be a written record and once adopted it must be followed. Too often, however, companies do it backward. You should create the plan before you decide upon the possible investment choices or the process for choosing."

Investment Options

A good set of investment options, also called the lineup, has diversified choices, low fees, and high scores from a thorough analysis (I use sophisticated software to help in my analysis).

What's the right number of options? We asked Sharon.

> "Between ten and fifteen. Usually no more than fifteen. The Employee Retirement Security Act of 1974 (ERISA) requires only three—a growth option, a value option, and an income option. The range must be suitable for all the participants, not just top executives."

Is it prudent to keep everything with one mega-firm that offers the gamut of products?

"A plan should be diversified, including more than one investment manager."

What about educating the participants?

"First you need experienced advisors. It is necessary to educate the plan sponsor [the boss, HR and possibly an investment committee]. Remember, managing the plan is not their day job. They're busy. I've never heard a plan sponsor say with glee, 'All right. It's time for a financial plan meeting. Let's go spend two hours in a room.'"

"What kinds of educational materials are used depends upon the workforce. Very few employees are likely to show up for an annual meeting. Possibilities include workshops, online videos, brochures, classroom or one-on-one sessions. American Funds offers brochures that cover topics like investing early versus investing late, or the difference that periodically increasing the contribution percentage makes. Classroom and one-on-one sessions are the most effective because it is possible to see when an employee has that 'aha moment.'"

Monitoring? Is it different for the individual participant and the investment committee?

"Yes. The individual participant should set aside the statements for a while. Looking at monthly or quarterly statements is just going on a roller coaster ride. The committee may want to monitor semiannually. How is an investment option doing against its benchmark? For very good fund families, monitoring annually may be enough."

Education

It seems logical that a good education is key to delivering a great 401(k) experience. Financial education is one of the top requests by employees and plan sponsors.

Some experts feel that the education service component should be separate from the investment component. Why? Because it is difficult to find a good education provider who is also a fiduciary.

> "Selecting an education and/or advice provider is a fiduciary decision," says Mark Dixon of Plante Moran financial advisors. "A plan sponsor [owner] should consider all of its options, including an independent provider.
>
> "By isolating the education process from the investment process, plan participants are receiving sound retirement education stripped of any sales motivation—removing any potential for conflicts of interest or liability from the organization's perspective . . . it is up to the plan fiduciary to monitor the education program to ensure that it's not sales driven. Turning to an independent provider substantially reduces this risk."[8]

It seems to be a far better solution to have a fiduciary advisor who brings an excellent education program to the plan. But of course, I'm biased.

I've been conducting financial education programs for more than twenty years and, as a Registered Investment Advisor, can provide advice.

---

[8] Mark Dixon. Plante Moran financial advisors. March 1, 2017. "Helping Retirement Plan Participants Prepare for the Future." https://www.plantemoran.com/explore-our-thinking/insight/2017/03/helping-retirement-plan-participants-prepare-for-the-future.

Monitoring the 401(k) Plan

Without monitoring, how do you know your 401(k) plan still fits your business?

Monitoring is quite important. To quote once again from Insperity.com's "5 Common Problems with Small Business Retirement Plans:"

> "As your business changes, your needs change. From 2009 to 2010 [a time of pronounced layoffs and business retrenchment], 14 percent of small businesses had never reviewed their retirement benefits, compared to 2 percent of large businesses, according to the annual Transamerica Retirement Survey. What your business was when you first adopted your company's pension plan might be completely different from what it is today. Be sure you're not paying for a plan that no longer suits your business."

How Does Your 401(k) Score?

It's important to know how your plan scores. Why? As a leader in your company you know how important it is to regularly evaluate employee performance. Your 401(k) is no different.

In fact, the Department of Labor (who regulates 401(k) plans) requires you to be a fiduciary. What does that mean? That means you are responsible for regularly evaluating your 401(k) and taking action when necessary. How do you do that?

It's actually easier than you think. You can use free online resources like www.401k-Score.com. How does this website work? Typically you'll enter your 401(k) sponsor's name and receive a report scoring your plan. The "report card" on your plan will come back with the equivalent of "Excellent, Fair, or Poor".

Can You Save Your 401(k) Plan Money?

A 401(k) is not free. There are numerous categories of expenses. It is possible for the plan sponsor or the fund pay the service fees, but commonly each participant pays a fee based on their investment choices and their share of the plan's overhead. Therefore, it's important to know how much your plan costs.

How Does Your 401(k) Score?

Excellent, Fair or Poor?

It's important to know how your plan scores. Why? As a leader in your company you know how important it is to regularly evaluate employee performance. Your 401(k) is no different.

In fact, the Department of Labor (who regulates 401(k) plans) requires you to be a fiduciary. What does that mean? That means you are responsible for regularly evaluating your 401(k) and taking action when necessary. How do you do that?

It's actually easier than you think. You can use free online resources like www.401k-Score.com. How do these work? Typically you'll enter your 401(k) sponsor's name and receive a report scoring your plan. The "report card" on your plan will come back with the equivalent of "Excellent," "Fair," or "Poor."

Summary: Regulations require ongoing evaluation of your plan, and for you to take action when necessary. Go to www.401k-Score.com to have your plan reviewed.

Plan fees and expenses are often hard to find. When you do find them, how do you even know if they're reasonable or not?

If you are your plan's fiduciary, you have the responsibility to review all plan costs. How do you do this? It's easy. It's called benchmarking your 401(k).

When you benchmark your 401(k) you will receive an analysis comparing your plan against those in your industry. A Plan benchmark report analyzes all critical areas of your 401(k), including investment performance, investment fees, bookkeeping, administration, and advisory costs.

How do you start the benchmarking process? You can use free online resources such as www.401k-Benchmark.com, where typically you will provide your form 408(b)2 (fee disclosure) and an asset statement.

Regulations require ongoing evaluation of your plan, and for you to take action when necessary.

Why Your Employees Hate Their 401(k)

Employers are often unaware of how their employees feel about the company's 401(k) plan. They don't understand why so many workers are not actively participating, not even to capture the matching contribution. They wonder why so few turn out for the educational seminars. It's baffling how employees are silent for so long, then one person makes a discovery and the HR department gets a stream of complaints.

This section is written firsthand from the perspective of a 401(k) participant who got the run around.

Anna, who is age sixty, works for a Northwest company with about 350 employees. She was silent, too, about her current employer's plan until she made a discovery. It involved in-service distributions. These withdrawals, by employees over age fifty-nine-

and-one-half who continue to work, can be done without penalty. Some plans allow them, and some do not.

Anna's Discovery Story in Her Own Words:

I signed up for my 401(k) at work when I was eligible after working for the organization for one year so that I could receive the employer matching benefit. When I signed up, I called the customer service line to verify that I could take out funds at age sixty because I wanted the flexibility to invest it elsewhere. I was told I could take funds out at age fifty-nine-and-one-half. During the next couple years, I saved the largest amount I was eligible for, including the catch-up amount for people over fifty. After contributing and reading my statements for three years, I turned sixty and decided to take out some funds, so I called the customer service line to find out how to do it.

I had attended the annual 401(k) informational meeting the first year I started contributing funds. The representative, who I understood was from a firm with a name that sounded like a bottled water brand, described the benefit and how it worked. She did not seem especially confident in what she was describing and was unable to answer questions from the employees attending. In short, she could move through the PowerPoint slides, but when asked questions, the answers never clicked in. Since I didn't think I gained much from the meeting, I didn't attend another.

At age sixty, when I decided to take the money out, I needed to find the contact information. I looked on our work shared drives to locate the 401(k) documents and found a "Participant Fee Disclosure Notice." I found a one-page "Plan Highlights" and a nineteen-page "Plan Description."

I dialed the 800 number for customer service I found on the Participant Fee Disclosure Notice. The instructions said to press zero to bypass the automated system. The recording said to enter my account number. I don't have an account number that I know of, so I pressed zero. I then was in an endless loop of being asked for the account number and pressing zero. Next, I found an email address on the same document, so I sent an email saying the phone was not working. I got a response with a local phone number. I called and it was answered quickly by a representative who identified herself as customer service for XYZ Corporation. I said I was trying to reach a different company. She explained they had been the same organization for years and were just getting around to changing their name. I asked her about the 800 number. She said they were having IT problems and were working on it.

How could I withdraw funds from my 401(k) to invest elsewhere?

She had to check first, then told me I wasn't eligible to take the salary deferrals out until I retired but I could take out the matching contributions. Puzzled, I asked her to send me the document she was looking at.

The next day she emailed me the Plan, a nineteen-page document, and the Plan Highlights, a single-page document. In the Plan Highlights, under the heading "In-Service Distribution," it said, "After having attained age fifty-nine-and-one-half or normal retirement age, a participant may withdraw all or a portion of his/her 100 percent vested account." I then checked the Plan Document. (The Plan Highlights noted that "the Plan Document supersedes all other communications.")

I called her back using the 800 number, which was on her email. It still didn't work. I called the local number and asked about the discrepancy between the documents. She replied that the information on the Plan Highlights was a mistake. I asked who created that document. She said that my employer wrote it.

I asked if she was an Accredited Investment Advisor. She said no, "but I've been doing this a long time." I asked her if anyone there was an AIA. She said "Yes, someone is." The question led to twenty minutes on hold before she came back with a name. When I looked him up I found a LinkedIn page saying he was an "Accredited Independent Fiduciary." Are they the same? (I have no idea)

I was losing confidence each step of the way, so I made a stab at finding out the plan's administrative fees. The customer service rep said she didn't think there were any administrative costs. Someone I know in the financial industry told me that didn't sound right. He suggested I ask for a copy of the Administrative Fee Disclosure or what is called a 408(b)2. Reading from my scribbled notes, I did. The rep told me my employer had that form.

I emailed my HR staff. They eventually replied:

"The info in the 408(b)2 is between [your employer] and Schwab [the brokerage firm involved]. I have requested a copy from Schwab, and will let you know when it is in.

"Do you have any more specifics on what you are asking for in regard to revenue-sharing information?"

I had started from a low base of knowledge but had learned that revenue-sharing is money that firms selling financial products such as mutual funds divide with the company responsible for holding my fund. Hmm. Would a doctor accept revenue sharing from a pharmaceutical company for writing prescriptions for its products?

A glutton for punishment, I had also emailed the custodian for our money, the firm whose name reminds me of the dog food jingles. The executive vice president of retirement services sent this email:

"Thanks for your questions ... I thought it might be easier if I sent you a list of funds, the expense ratio of each fund in the plan, and the revenue-sharing percentage, if applicable.

"In most cases revenue sharing goes to the broker or person who sells you the fund. Since we are an independent investment advisor, we do not want that money and do not keep it. In the case of your plan the revenue sharing goes to pay Charles Schwab for their third-party custodial and trustee services. The amount generated from those four funds pays all the Charles Schwab costs each year. This is generally a cost that is borne by most plan participants.

"The revenue sharing is not an additional cost; it is included in the expense ratio of the fund ...

"Compared with many other plans [your employer's] 401(k) Plan [sic] has an investment line-up with exceptionally low expenses; in fact, the simple average is just 0.33 percent, but you could also go rock bottom in terms of cost with your own allocation by creating a portfolio with only Vanguard and DFA funds. There is a lot of flexibility for you to customize your own allocation and we are also available to provide investment advice if you need help."

The email had an attachment that listed the funds, expense ratio and the revenue sharing ratio.

One month later, I had learned more on my own than I ever could from some young agent speaking to us in my employer's cafeteria. Yet, I still had not heard back about a copy of the 408(b)2.

I later found documents that showed that the plan had changed the in-service distribution requirements the previous year. I don't recall being notified of that.

In talking to co-workers over lunch, I realize there is a generation gap, the opposite of the one where older people who didn't grow up with the new technology struggle. With retirement plans, people in their thirties and forties are having a hard time just paying their bills. The financial provisions are confusing, and retirement seems so far away. For those of us in our fifties and sixties, retirement is close. It's still confusing but we are learning about what is in our best interests. We know more than the next generation.

MORAL

Just one seemingly isolated case still can be a danger signal. If a company is paying attention, it can lead to a review that shows just how broken the firm's retirement plan, or plan administration, really is.

Being aware of the common mistakes is the first step. Our next chapter will focus on how to overcome them.

CHAPTER THREE

Overcoming 401(k) Mistakes in Four Easy Steps

Knowing about common 401(k) mistakes can help you avoid them (at least, most of them). Correcting the inevitable bobble depends upon a moment of discovery. You have to know what is broken, and why, before you can fix it.

> It is not hard to predict how the story ends for the employee who wants to make a penalty-free withdrawal—an in-service distribution—against the background of the company changing its rules and word not being delivered to those who need to know.

In the previous chapter, it seems pretty evident that Anna got the run around. No one person took personal responsibility.

The mega-brokerage firm, involved on the investment side, says this is an internal company matter. The outside firm acting as advisor appears to be less than proactive. The harried human resources representative likely will become immersed in day-to-day issues and follow up may be their lowest priority. The employee, to whom this question is very important, will have to keep nagging.

Given the confusion in Anna's case, perhaps the company could have granted a one-time exception for the employee to make the withdrawal (they didn't). After all, if the IRS has no problem with it, why should the company? Given that three firms are involved—plan sponsor, plan custodian (the brokerage) and plan advisor—"sorry, ask someone else" is the more likely result.

How about a pragmatic, informal solution to dealing with employee questions? Human resources should catalog the types of questions or problems presented and assign each case a number, a less-rigorous version of what the information technology folks do, such as: case seventeen opened on X date, was resolved on Y date.

In-service distributions for those fifty-nine-and-one-half years and up are not even on the radar screen of millennials, now still in their twenties and thirties.

This near-retiree, however, quite likely will spill her story to co-workers at the lunch table, and it is more than a withdrawal story now. She is concerned about fees and believes she can handle her own money herself at lower cost and with better results than the current three companies involved.

How long before HR starts getting more inquiries piling up?

This case, certainly not a common one, involves mistakes in three areas:

• The plan document was changed, but not updated in the highlights document;

• The plan advisor was not properly monitoring, to see that changes were enacted appropriately with all parties being informed;

• And, regarding education, those in the first line of communication at the company level were not kept in the loop.

Unfortunately, this is more common than what we'd like to hear about.

Let's not be too harsh on Anna's company. Sharon Pivirotto, the professional I quoted earlier who trains plan advisors and who writes a 401(k) blog (401kbestpractices.com), points out:

> "Many companies and benefit plans are small enough that creating a formal committee for plan oversight is not a viable option. As companies grow and plan assets increase, formalizing the committee structure makes more sense."

That seems to be the case here. Retirement programs can be set up by the boss and another employee who is probably the entire HR department. They often use data from a couple of outside firms who may have been found on a casual word-of-mouth referral instead of by a formal request for proposal.

As an advisor, I offer a holistic solution to companies with existing retirement programs that addresses the three key aspects mentioned above. I hate getting the runaround myself, and I sure wouldn't stand for one of my plan participants to be treated the way Anna was.

What Do You Do Next?

Evaluate your existing plan. Is there a fiduciary advising you? Are the fees low? Does the plan have a brokerage option with both autopilot choices such as target date and index funds, and also include self-managed-with-guidance choices (international, alternative investments, sector, and actively managed funds)?

If the fees are high and your plan does not have a brokerage option, there is every reason for employees to take an in-service distribution (moving assets out of the plan), so they can have more control. Remember, these are employees trying to play catch-up who realize retirement is just over the horizon. They want to save more, but they also want their money to work harder.

My basic model has low fees, no transaction charges, and available in-service distributions. It includes educational seminars and one-on-one sessions offered by a financial industry veteran, not a PowerPoint clicker.

Four Common 401(k) Mistakes

The four common retirement mistakes companies make involve:
1. Investment Policy Statement
2. Investment Options
3. Monitoring
4. Education

Can You Save Your 401(k) Plan Money?
Be the 401(k) Champion

A 401(k) is not free. There are numerous categories of expenses. Each participant pays a fee based on their investment choices and their share of the plan's overhead. Therefore, it's important to know how much your plan costs.

Plan fees and expenses are often hard to find. When you do find them, how do you even know if they're reasonable or not?

If you are your plan's fiduciary, you have the responsibility to review all plan costs. How do you do this? It's easy. It's called benchmarking your 401(k).

When you benchmark your 401(k) you will receive an analysis comparing your plan against those in your industry. A plan benchmark report analyzes all critical areas of your 401(k), including investment performance, investment fees, bookkeeping, administration, and advisory costs.

How do you start the benchmarking process? You can use free online resources such as www.401k-Benchmark.com. How do these work? Typically, you'll provide your form 408(b)2 (fee disclosure) and an asset statement. If you're unfamiliar with those documents, call your current plan fiduciary or my office at 206-362-0503.

Summary: Regulations require ongoing evaluation of your plan, and for you to take action when necessary. Go to www.401k-Benchmark.com to have your plan benchmarked for free.

Investment Policy Statement

The investment policy statement is kind of a "Which comes first, the chicken or the egg?" question. Some advisors prefer to craft the plan document first. The investment policy statement (IPS) is the overall guide, setting forth the goals, which parties are responsible for what, and the philosophy or criteria for the investment portfolio.

The investment policy statement needs to be specific enough to have meaning, and flexible enough to accommodate changes that the future brings. Once adopted, the plan needs to follow the IPS and revise it if necessary.

Of course, there are some investment policy statements and financial software that advisors can use in building the policy statement. It need not be as tedious as writing your firm's mission statement, sweating over each word, or designing the logo that will symbolically define you in the public's mind for decades to come.

I prefer to come up with the menu of investment options first, while keeping in the back of my mind the type of company and the sophistication of its workforce.

Investment Options

There are as many investment options out there as college choices confronting your high school senior.

Pity the poor boss or small investment committee trying to come up with a seat-of-their-pants list of investment choices while tending to their day jobs. Financial advisors have the edge, both in financial training and experience and modern financial software tools at their disposal.

In the financial version of decision making, there are stock and bond funds, domestic and international companies, companies with various sizes of market capitalization (small cap, mid cap, large cap), growth or value companies, passive investments that mimic an index, or actively managed funds that try to beat the market.

The mistakes to avoid or overcome are too few choices (putting employees in a straitjacket), or so many options that employees are overwhelmed. Other big mistakes are staying with just one fund family or choosing funds with expensive fees.

Some advisors feel that twelve to fifteen choices are ample. There is no right answer. The categories just ticked off could amount to a dozen funds. Add in target date growth or income funds spaced five years apart and there are a dozen more.

I favor coming up with a preferred menu while giving employees who wish to do so a brokerage option by going off the reservation to other respected funds. Passive or active? Vegan or meat? I want to come up with a menu with choices for all.

Again, the pros—fiduciaries who put the participants' interests first—have the advantage. I can select twelve investment criteria such as performance, style, fees and such. Then I search for funds without problems in any of the criteria. Financial software enables me to do the search again and again at the touch of a button.

Meanwhile, the financial committee who opted for a "DIY approach," locked in a conference room, is muttering in debate as work piles up at their desks.

Monitoring

The world changes, and so do investments. On a scale of zero to one hundred, with zero representing no problems, the goal in crafting a menu is for funds with zeros across the board.

With time, problems may result from style drift, a fund deviating from large caps to small or domestic to foreign, or putting up miserable performance on any of the twelve criteria.

I get an alert any time a fund creeps above twenty-five on the scale.

Fiduciary advisors can act one of two ways: An advisor who makes changes to the plan is called a 3(38) advisor. An advisor who only makes recommendations to a plan sponsor is called a 3(21) advisor.

As a 3(38), or higher-discretion advisor, I analyze and verify, and make a substitution if warranted. Contrast that with a 3(21) or lower-level, make-suggestions advisor who may come to the same conclusion but must wait for an investment committee to schedule a meeting and decide.

A plan sponsor without sophisticated technology may be like a boat with a broken rudder, drifting far off course. That is, of course, a mistake.

Educate

The shift from traditional pensions, with the employer being on the hook for retirement finances, to 401(k)s where the employee bears all the responsibility, has come within the span of a working career.

That is a short time for a major social change. Surveys and short quizzes show workers and executives alike typically are not financially savvy. They never had a class in high school or college on the costs of everyday living, the toll of inflation over decades, or how much must be stashed away for an expected long life amid ever-rising medical expenses.

Employees—at least those who expect to have enough disposable income to be able to save—want to be educated. They want to know more than the mundane details of how to fill out a participation form or when the company's match is invested. They may not want to master "Investments 401" and become a self-directed investor. Yet it would be nice to have some guidance regarding which of several assortments from the plan's menu of choices might be recommended for them, based on their age, family situation, salary and net worth, and attitude toward risk. In the May 21, 2015 article, "Employees Want Help Deciding How Much to Save," Stephen Miller cites a Northern Trust Survey that employees overwhelmingly favor their employers' playing a larger role in helping them save for retirement.[9]

The survey of more than 1,000 participants in workplace 401(k)s or other defined-contribution retirement plans found:

- 88 percent of participants strongly or somewhat strongly favor their employers' providing tools to help determine if they are saving the correct amount for a financially secure retirement.
- 80 percent believe employers should encourage employees to contribute to their retirement plan, and 84 percent support employers' providing incentives to encourage contributions.
- 72 percent think employers should provide a viewpoint on contribution amounts.

In addition, more than four in five employees surveyed said they would consider taking their employer's advice when determining the size of their contribution to a 401(k) plan.

Employers Want Their Employees to Have Great Education on Investing and Retirement

The study also found employers—the plan sponsors—are reluctant to take a more active role in encouraging specific levels of saving or projecting retirement income for reasons of liability. Much of that liability, however, can be passed off by hiring an

---

[9] Stephen Miller. SHRM.org. May 21, 2015. "Employees Want Help Deciding How Much to Save." (Northern Trust Survey conducted by Mathew Greenwald, Greenwald & Associates).
https://www.shrm.org/resourcesandtools/hr-topics/benefits/pages/savings-contributions.aspx

outside advisor who has fiduciary status. We'll explain that in a future chapter.

Advisors can provide help at two levels, as I referenced earlier. According to the IRS codes, a 3(21) advisor can compile and suggest a list of menu choices, for example. A 3(38) advisor compiles the list, gets some input from the company as the plan sponsor, but ultimately makes the decision. It is similar with the process of educating employees.

I prefer to act as a 3(38), a higher-level advisor. I am a fiduciary, so tell me what you think you would like and leave it to me.

It is similar with the education process. In a 3(21) arrangement, the company is responsible for the education. Company executives have no particular expertise and fear liability, so generally participants receive little or no education, save for an outside brochure or two, a video, or maybe that PowerPoint presentation—just don't ask the person doing the clicking to answer questions.

In more than two decades of educational presentations, I've found that employees want face-to-face contact. Oh sure, I can point them to pamphlets, videos, and online readings if need be. I don't hear any clamoring for that, however.

Typically, I come to a client company twice a year for seminars with all employees as well as to have thirty-minute meet-and-greet sessions in private with each participant who wishes to do so.

The classes address the broad concepts such as always diversify, stage of life, anticipated level of replacement income necessary in retirement, long-term care, and life expectancy. The concept questions don't change much, but the timely questions do.

Say the stock market has been dropping for several weeks:

"Should I pull my money out, or put it into cash or bonds?"

The answer: It is best not to get emotional. People who pull out their money invariably wait too long before putting it back in. They miss the ride up. If you're in your mid-thirties, you have thirty years before you will need those savings. With each paycheck, you are buying stocks or other financial products at a discount. Five years from now, thirty years from now, in my opinion, your investments are likely to grow. It is your decision. I suggest staying the course.

The individual sessions tend to be short and sweet because I know employees have their work duties on their mind. I often say, "We can stretch this out for two or more visits lasting two hours each on Saturdays. Or we can cut to the chase, find out your goals, your salary and savings levels, how much time until you need the money, and how you feel about risk. We can get you out of here and going about your life in thirty minutes." Participants are quick to choose the express lane.

A Personal Fiduciary Advisor Makes the Team Stronger

Take Charles Schwab as an example. They have experienced tremendous growth because they make it easy for independent fiduciaries to use their technology.

Charles Schwab & Co., which is often ranked as the second-largest broker in the country, salutes the nation's independent financial advisors.

The giant brokerage and financial services firm has been airing television commercials praising and explaining the role of the independents, one of the fastest-growing segments of the financial industry. Schwab has even created a website, findyourindependentadvisor.com.

Schwab says it is the largest supporter of the independent advisors, which by some estimates have $6.9 trillion of client wealth entrusted to them.

The campaign does not recommend specific advisors. It does arm consumers with information to guide them in seeking qualified assistance and in asking the right questions before establishing a relationship.

To be sure, this campaign is aimed at consumers—those in need of advice and assistance across the entire spectrum of financial topics. The focus of this book is on 401(k) plan formation and administration. It is directed at companies (the plan sponsors) and employee participants desiring more robust plan choices and better results at lower costs.

Schwab profits from the sales of financial products and wealth-management services. So, it is remarkable to hear the mega-firm beating the drums for the model of independent advisors to supply guidance and contacts with clients while a custodian such as Schwab holds the money in accounts and handles financial transactions, recordkeeping, and other operational aspects.

That is also the model espoused in this book, to relieve companies of the burden of administering 401(k) plans, reducing their legal exposure, cutting fees, and offering more personalized service to employees.

So, let's hear what Schwab has to say without any prompting from the multitude of independent advisors across the land.

Benefits of Having an Independent Advisor

The benefits of having independent advisors are listed by Schwab as:

- *They are not tied to a particular family of funds or investment products.*

- *As fiduciaries, the independent advisors are held to the highest standard of care.*

- *Fiduciaries are required to act in the best interests of clients at all times.*

- *The independent advisors (fiduciaries) are registered with the Securities and Exchange Commission or state securities regulators.*

But wait, there's more.

Additional benefits cited by Schwab:

- *Independent advisors can provide customized guidance.*

- *A smaller, involved party leads to a relationship that is responsive, attentive and personal.*

- *The arrangement has a simple and transparent fee structure.*

- *The advisors provide a high level of expertise. (Schwab's website even takes a stab at taking some mystery out of the jungle of financial acronyms—see the following "Who's Who?" section.)*

- *The division of labor means your money is held by an independent custodian, not the advisor firm. There are several advantages in the separation of responsibilities, including concentration in focus and an additional check and balance.*

Ever Wonder Who's Who?[10]

CFP: Certified Financial Planner. Holders of the credential typically have completed university-level financial coursework and passed a ten-hour exam on ninety topics.

CFA: Chartered Financial Analyst. These are people who have passed three exams, given a year apart, and each requiring a minimum of 250 hours of study.

PFS: Personal Financial Specialist. These are certified public accountants (CPAs) who specialize in personal financial planning.

CIMA: Certified Investment Management Analyst. These credential holders specialize in asset allocation and usually have completed coursework at the University of California (Berkeley) or the University of Pennsylvania (Wharton School).

Summary

With a financial mechanism as complex as a 401(k), you're bound to encounter mishaps. While it's important to know how to correct those mistakes, it's *more* important to be able to spot potential issues ahead of time and correct course to avoid them in the first place. As they say, an ounce of prevention is worth a pound of cure. Keeping your employees engaged with education and selecting an investment advisor are just a few ways to stay on top of your duty.

---

[10] Charles Schwab & Co., Inc.

CHAPTER FOUR

Let the IPS Be Your GPS

Little did we dream when the first Sputnik was launched in 1957 that global positioning systems would be commonplace a half century later in our cars or cell phones. The global positioning system, or GPS, guides us to destinations where we have never been before.

The GPS can tell us the shortest route, the quickest route, the nearest gasoline station, or Italian restaurant along the way. The GPS is well on its way to making the road map obsolete and has saved countless men the embarrassment of having to stop and ask a stranger for directions.

In the 401(k) universe, the investment policy statement, or IPS, keeps us on the right course, monitors our progress, and gets us to our destination, if we follow it. It is like a road map, only better.

An IPS Is Not Required But It Is a "Best Practice"

Technically, the Internal Revenue Service and the Department of Labor does not mandate that sponsors of 401(k) plans have an investment policy statement. Outside advisors, however, rightly urge their fiduciary clients to adopt a formal IPS setting forth the goals and procedures for selecting, monitoring, and replacing investments.

In practice, adopting a policy and not following it can be worse than not having a written policy at all. The Department of Labor considers the policy one of the instruments and documents governing the plan, which means that mere failure to follow the IPS can be a fiduciary breach. More important, failure to follow the IPS will likely result in your participants having a suboptimum investment menu.

For openers, the policy statement defines the role of the investment committee, sets forth an investment philosophy, and provides guidance on what investments should be included. It describes how and when progress should be monitored.

The statement can be a safeguard. Once in place, it can provide evidence that the plan sponsor is dutifully acting as a fiduciary in overseeing investments.

So, how do you create an investment policy statement, an integral step in offering or strengthening a retirement tax shelter program in the workplace?

Research shows that 90 percent of defined-contribution plans, aka 401(k)s, have investment policy statements, says Healy Jones, head of marketing for the ForUsAll 401(k) Blog.

7 Aspects of an Investment Policy Statement

Jones suggests seven aspects that should be considered:
- Plan purpose—why the plan exists
- Investment objectives/capabilities
- Guidance on monitoring investments
- The asset classes that will be included
- Instructions on selecting investments, the approach to performance and measuring results
- Establishment of a default fund (A default fund is for when a contributor does not provide instructions on where to place

funds. ForUsAll, Jones says, typically uses low-cost target date funds in those situations.)

• Participant education (By spelling out the requirements for employee education, the IPS can increase the likelihood that participants or prospective participants know how the plan works.)

What to Avoid

Fiduciary Plan Governance, LLC is a firm headquartered in Newbury, Massachusetts, which provides guidance and other services. It counsels investment committees and advisors to avoid extreme detail or vagueness. Instead, strike a balance.

Don't be too specific in describing the command structure, advises FPG. Responsibilities can and should be delegated to outside people or organizations, but they do not have to be mentioned by name in the policy statement.

Don't omit a contingency plan, the firm advises. In the event of a market crash, banking meltdown or other extreme situation, the investment policy statement needs to give the plan sponsor team the ability to evaluate and take appropriate action in a timely manner.

Samples for a model investment policy statement are available from several firms and organizations. Morgan Stanley has a sample at www.morganstanleyfa.com. So does T. Rowe Price at www.troweprice.com. Fi360.com, which helps financial intermediaries, also weighs in with one.

We chose a sample IPS from 401khelpcenter.com, a knowledge and resource service based in Portland, Oregon. Rick Meigs, president, granted permission to reprint the sample below.

Sample IPS

Investment Policy Statement for the XYZ 401(k) Profit-Sharing Plan

Summary of Plan Information

Plan Sponsor: XYZ, Inc.

Plan Name: XYZ 401(k) Profit-Sharing Plan

Date This Policy Statement Adopted: February 11, 2003.

Statement of Purpose for the Policy and the Plan

The XYZ 401(k) Profit Sharing Plan ("Plan") is a defined-contribution retirement plan available to all eligible employees. The Plan's purpose is to provide a cash or deferred arrangement for Plan participants (for the purposes of this document, participants will include beneficiaries and any parties in interest as defined within ERISA). Investment of Plan assets will be made for the sole interest and exclusive purpose of providing benefits to participants. It is the intent of the Investment Committee ("Committee") [Insert name of your committee or board of directors or board of trustees depending on the makeup of your Plan administration] to provide a range of investment options that will enable participants to invest according to varying risk tolerance, savings time horizon, and other financial goals.

The Plan's investment funds will be selected and monitored with the skill, care and diligence that a prudent individual acting in a like capacity would undertake and in accordance with all other aspects of applicable law, including the requirements of the Employee Retirement Income Security Act of 1974 (ERISA), as amended, and Sections 401(a) and 501(a) of the Internal Revenue Code of 1986 (Code), as amended. The Plan is intended to qualify under the qualified cash or deferred arrangement rules of Code Section 401(k). The Plan is a participant directed individual account plan that it is intended to comply as a "404(c) Plan" within the meaning of the Department of Labor Regulations under ERISA Section 404(c) and as such, it provides individual accounts for Plan participants to select how these individual accounts shall be invested and therefore, no fiduciary shall be liable for any loss that results from a participant's exercise of control over the investment of his or her participant accounts.

The purpose of the document is to provide the Committee with guidance in discharging certain fiduciary responsibilities. It creates no obligation to act in any way. The Committee will monitor all of the evaluation criteria as well as any other material issues when making decisions concerning the Plan's investment funds. To maximize diversification and lessen risk to the extent possible, the Plan offers a balanced portfolio of investment funds composed of equity, fixed income, and cash-equivalent securities, and, as such, is intended to be more aggressive than fixed income portfolios and less aggressive than purely equity-oriented portfolios.

The Plan offers a broad range of diversified investments that will enable a participant to construct a portfolio with aggregate risk and return characteristics at any point within the participant's desired range. Adherence to the specific investment objectives and criteria contained herein will be evaluated over a full market cycle, which historically has been five to seven years. The Committee may, from time to time as warranted, modify these objectives and criteria according to the Committee's discretion in consultation with such financial advisors as it deems appropriate.

Because participants in the Plan ultimately are responsible for their own investment decisions, the Committee aims to provide participants with the following capabilities:

Choose from a minimum of five diverse alternative investment fund categories, each with materially different risk and return characteristics, at least one of which will provide for a high degree of safety and capital preservation.

Make investment decisions at least quarterly.

Receive or have access to the following information in accordance with ERISA Section 404(c) (Please refer to ERISA Section 404(c) for a complete list of information that participants will receive), as updated:

A description of the investment alternatives available under the Plan including a general description of the investment objectives, risk and return characteristics, and type and diversification of assets comprising each alternative;

A description of any transaction fees or expenses charged to the participant's account, and information on fund costs and fees that reduce the rate of return to participants (expense ratios); and

Fund prospectuses, annual reports, and semiannual reports.

A description of how, when, and to whom participants may give investment instructions or identification of designated investment managers.

Protection of capital gains to obtain a positive return over a given market-cycle.

Asset growth, exclusive of contributions and withdrawals, should exceed the rate of inflation to preserve purchasing power.

Obtain stable and consistent returns.

Approach to Performance and Measurement

When selecting investment options, each investment manager must meet certain minimum criteria:

They must be a bank, insurance company or investment management company or an investment adviser under the Investment Advisers Act of 1940.

They must be operating in good standing with regulators and clients, with no material pending or concluded legal actions.

They must provide detailed additional information on the history of the firm, its investment philosophy and approach, and its principals, clients, locations, fee schedules, and other relevant information.

The Retirement Plan Investment Committee will review the investment objectives and risk characteristics, historical performance, and expenses related to each available Plan investment option and choose a specific option based on these procedures and objectives. The Committee recognizes that risk, volatility, and the possibility of loss in purchasing power are present to some degree in all types of investment vehicles. While high levels of risk are to be avoided, the assumption of risk is warranted and encouraged to allow the Committee the opportunity to achieve satisfactory long-term results consistent with these procedures and objectives.

Generally, all investment options are expected to perform as well as or better than their prescribed performance standards, net of fees. In any case, the Committee shall have full discretion and reserves the right to offer or terminate an investment option at any time, for any reason. Once the decision to terminate an investment option is made, asset transfer and liquidation should be handled to the best advantage of the plan.

Monitoring of Investment Options

The ongoing monitoring of investments will be a regular and disciplined process. While frequent change is neither expected nor desirable, the process of monitoring investment performance relative to specified guidelines is an ongoing process.

The Committee will review periodically the investment managers' progress in meeting the Plan's investment objectives on at least a quarterly basis. The Board of Directors will review the Plan's investment offerings and the Committee's actions pertaining to investment options at least once per year. Generally, the Committee realizes investment managers should be given a full market cycle to achieve stated objectives, therefore greater weight will be given to market-cycle performance than performance in any given year. However, the Committee recognizes that economic, political, social, or other changes could occur requiring action sooner than a full-market cycle. Investment options that consistently under-perform in terms of risk and return will be carefully reviewed to determine if any action is warranted.

Default Investment Fund Selection

For those participants who fail to give investment instructions regarding either their balance in the Plan or future contributions to the Plan, the Committee has determined that such balances and contributions will be invested in a Qualified Default Investment Alternative (QDIA) as described in US Department of Labor regulations. The Committee, with the assistance of the plan recordkeeper where appropriate, will:

Select a [insert type of investment fund] as the default investment option under the Plan.

Notify each participant thirty days in advance of the initial investment and annually thereafter with a description of the investment, the participant's rights to change the investment and how to obtain additional information or to make changes.

Allow the participant to provide the opportunity to direct investments in its account any time prior to or after the placement of funds in the QDIA.

On an ongoing basis provide the same level of information as the other investment options in the Plan.

In conducting these activities, the Committee will follow the requirements of the Plan's ERISA Section 404(c) Policy Statement.

Participant Investment Education

In developing a continual participant investment education program, the Plan will select funds and provide supporting material with consideration for the following:

The number of funds offered should be limited to promote participant understanding without sacrificing the objectives set forth in this policy.

The Plan Sponsor should provide general information relating to the economy and capital markets as part of the investment education program.

Participants should be encouraged to select an appropriate asset allocation (based on their risk tolerance, their time until retirement and other factors relating to their personal financial status) and avoid attempts to time the market.

The Plan Sponsor should educate participants on the relative risk and return of investing in different asset classes and how diversified investing can reduce the risk of investing.

Coordination with the Plan Document

Notwithstanding the foregoing, if any term or condition of this investment policy conflicts with any term or condition in the Plan, the terms and conditions of the Plan shall control.

ON BEHALF OF XYZ INC. 401(K) PROFIT SHARING PLAN:

Name:

Title:

Date:

Taking the Census of America's 401(k) Plans

Like pencil marks on a closet door frame recording a child's growth in height, Deloitte Consulting LLP has been cataloguing the emergence of America's 401(k) industry each year.

The fifteenth edition of "Defined Contribution Benchmarking Survey" surveyed 240 plan sponsors to provides tidbits and trends, some of them surprising.

Companies are concerned about participation levels and whether employees are saving enough for retirement as traditional pensions become rarer and rarer. In 2017, the executive summary of the latest survey reports, 35 percent of employers conducted retirement readiness assessments. This was up 23 percentage points from just three years earlier.

Plan sponsors are making more managed accounts available, signaling to participants that there is professional help available if they choose.

Some firms are reducing the number of menu choices, seeking to declutter and avoid overwhelming apprehensive workers. Contrarily, additional passive, lower-cost investments are being offered.

Here are a few of the results from the extensive survey:

Participation. Some 80 percent of employees participate today, with the median account balance at $97,440.

Fiduciary rule. Uncertainty about the Department of Labor's rule on fiduciaries with delays and phased-in implementation is a hot topic. Among plan sponsors, 57 percent express confidence about their understanding of their fiduciary responsibility while 37 percent said they are still reviewing the potential effects.

Making retirement preparation simpler. Of the firms in the report, 65 percent say they have added autopilot functions—

automatic enrollment, step-up contribution schedules and managed accounts—and 55 percent say they are simplifying the investment menu options.

Why employees participate. The leading responses are to take advantage of company matches (41 percent), personal desire to save for retirement (31 percent) and automatic enrollment (19 percent).

Why employees don't participate. The leading response is lack of awareness or understanding (28 percent).

Investment guidance. Companies are still leery of providing generic or broad investment counseling with 53 percent citing potential fiduciary liability, 33 percent saying employees are not interested and 25 percent being concerned about the cost.

Recruiting and retention. In the study, 74 percent of firms believe the 401(k) plan is an effective recruiting tool, and 62 percent feel it assists in retaining employees.[11]

We've talked about the investment policy statement, now let's discuss the actual investments themselves.

---

[11] Deloitte 2017 Defined Contribution Benchmarking Survey.
https://www.deloitte.com/us/en/pages/human-capital/articles/annual-defined-contribution-benchmarking-survey.html

CHAPTER FIVE

Create an All-Star Lineup of Investments

The difference between success and failure, or at least disappointingly mediocre results, often lies in the details.

Crafting an investment policy statement, as described in the previous chapter, is of paramount importance. Getting across the possible investment choices and what may be appropriate for a given employee are the subjects for the next chapter.

In between we have the details, such as choosing the investment options that will be available to a company's retirement program participants.

There are literally thousands of possible choices. Offer too few investment options, and participants may miss out on opportunities to see their investments grow and compound. Offer too many and participants, particularly those with little financial experience, will be overwhelmed and suffer investment paralysis, afraid to make any choice.

In our experience, it isn't about a perfect number of options as much as it is about having the perfect number of options for your staff. Staff members' comfort levels and interest will drive your optimal number and what an all-star lineup looks like to you.

How to Select Twenty from a Field of Thousands

First, start with the asset classes. Stock funds for growth. Exchange traded fundsare supplanting mutual funds in popularity for a variety of reasons, including lower fees. Passive stock funds, those tied to an index and offering extremely low fees, need to be in the lineup. So do target-date funds, which automatically change their asset mixes as participants age. Many employees like the lower volatility of bond funds. Those very close to retirement may have a need for money market funds or similar instruments with short-term holdings and stable prices. Alternative investments such as real estate investment trusts need to be considered. Allowing qualified participants to "go off the reservation" and choose individual stocks or funds not on the menu is a possible course, but one that needs to be discussed thoroughly with the plan sponsor.

There is another wrinkle as well. Some companies automatically enroll new hires at a modest level as a default, unless they specifically ask to be excluded. This allows them to capture some of the company match. What if the employee provides no direction on how to invest the money? That is called a Qualified Default Option with significant ramifications for plan sponsor and advisor (see box).

Before coming up with a list of twenty options, the independent advisor has to have in the back of his or her mind the type of workforce involved. He or she should be prepared to educate participants as to what is appropriate to their financial situation, stage of life, and the current phase of the economic cycle.

Is the workforce college educated and somewhat financially sophisticated, at least on the basics, or loaded with recent high school graduates earning entry-level wages? A young workforce has a long time horizon before the money is needed, whereas a middle-aged cohort may be more cautious, since retirement is on the horizon. Put another way, millennials are so different from baby boomers in attitudes, lifestyles, and financial approaches. What's wrong with the folks' basement?

It may sound complicated. Fortunately, the marriage of human expertise and discretion with modern computer software and databases makes it much less so. At my firm in Seattle, we start with the human element, coming up with the twelve most important criteria to use in judging a prospective stock, bond, or other investment vehicle.

Then comes the technology side. An organization called fi360 provides training and resources to independent advisors. Ask their database to rank possible choices based on the twelve criteria and the scores show up at lightning speed. If human due diligence suggests the top-ranked contender may not be appropriate for some reason, tweak the criteria and run the results again.

That isn't the only resource available to the independent advisors. In our case, we are allied with TD Ameritrade, so their research staff and computer power are available as well.

The task has been whittled down to manageable proportions. Times may change, however. The all-star lineup for next season may call for some new players. No problem. Give some thought to altering the criteria and press the computer button again.

When an Employee Cannot Decide

What to do when an employee cannot decide whether to participate in the company's 401(k) retirement plan?

Many companies, concerned that employees will not have enough money for retirement as traditional pensions vanish, automatically enroll new hires in the 401(k) defined contribution programs at a minimal level. That way they can capture some of the company match and take the first step toward systematically saving for retirement. Some companies even adopt an automatic increase feature, raising employee contributions in step with merit or experience raises.

What happens, however, when the employee fails to provide direction on how to invest the money? Where does it go?

There's a question of possible liability if the plan sponsor or advisor decide on the employee's behalf, says the online advisory service BUYandHOLDisdead.com. Many plan sponsors argue that a 2006 revision to ERISA provides a safe harbor protection.

There is confusion and some Department of Labor changes that would provide clarity are on hold until July 1, 2019.

The online advisory service quotes a Department of Labor Specialist that, to qualify for the safe harbor the 401(k), fiduciaries must do the following for participants:

- *Allow the opportunity to move their investments into an alternate account*

- *Provide advance notice of the default investment*

- *Invest the assets in certain kinds of qualified default investments*

Herbert A. Whitehouse, chief fiduciary officer at The Bogdahn Group of Orlando, Florida, says those typically are low volatility investments similar to money market funds, target-date funds, managed account target-date funds, and sometimes balanced funds.

In practice, the Rochester (New York) Regional Health Savings Plans solved the dilemma by simply selecting Vanguard Target Retirement Fund Institutional Shares as the default, effective July 1, 2017.

Changing regulations and regulatory uncertainty are reasons cited by plan sponsors when hiring experts to handle their programs.

Summary

We've discussed the investment options, so now we turn to education. Once you're comfortable that your 401(k) has an investment policy statement and a good lineup of investments, how do you implement a great education program?

CHAPTER SIX

If You Think Education Is Costly, You're Going to Hate Ignorance

By "education," we mean more than just the nuts and bolts of how to enroll, company matches and when they are vested, or the list of investment choices.

Some companies are reluctant to offer real education about their retirement programs, citing potential expense and legal liability. I think this is a mistake.

Great Education Increases Participation

The fears of not providing education, while fairly common, are groundless. Greater participation and contributions can be a win/win/win for providers, employees, and employers. Surely you've heard of "the fear of the unknown"? Increasing knowledge for employees can turn the unknown, foreign-sounding plan into a known and desired good.

A True Fiduciary Advisor's Goals Are Aligned with the Participant's Goals

Let's start with the providers, not that 401(k) programs exist for their benefit. If providers charge their fees based as a percentage of assets under management, they have a self-interest incentive in encouraging participation. The more employees who are participating, the more robust the level of contributions, the more positive the account growth, the higher the total of assets under management and the annual fees the providers collect.

Employees who participate are taking a step toward preparing for retirement and their own financial wellness. Lack of awareness, an overwhelming amount of investment choices, and fear of the stock market can intimidate employees from joining. Broad education can help them overcome their fears and participate. To the extent that entry- or low-level employees have discretionary income, a contribution is not an expense. In one sense, a dollar contributed does not really go away. Sure, it may leave their control and not be accessible for thirty or forty years, but it is still their money. It is an investment for their non-working years.

Employers, the owners, suffer from ignorance as well. They tend to have the highest incomes, the most discretionary income and the ability to contribute up to the maximums. High levels of administrative costs rob them the most as the money is diverted from going into the investment accounts and growing. All too often, the boss and even the human resources executive, don't comprehend why administrative costs matter or why the financial well-being of the employee is in the company's best interest, as well. That should not be surprising. They have a business to run; 401(k)s didn't even exist until four decades ago, and this major societal change is not fully ingrained on the public psyche. Education is often required.

A company's employees need and crave broad guidance and general information, such as the percentage contribution level that might reasonably assure a secure retirement; the relationship of risk and reward, and that the right balance depends upon the individual and the stage of life; a contribution at a youthful age—competing with so many wants and necessities—can compound much greater with ample passage of time.

There need not be fear of liability in providing general, nonspecific information about risk and return, diversification, and other investment concepts. Such general education is allowable and not subject to the fiduciary standard.

Think back to December 2007 through June 2009 and the nation's slide into the Great Recession. Layoffs mushroomed. Companies froze or even eliminated benefits. Housing prices took a swan dive and foreclosures soared. Meanwhile, the stock market tanked and employees saw their quarterly retirement balances shrivel and shrivel again.

For many, if not most, this was uncharted territory. What should they do? Should they switch all their investment money into cash, perhaps selling at the bottom? Should they reduce or quit contributing, only to pay a severe price twenty or thirty years later in retirement?

During the '08 Recession, Employees Cried Out for Guidance

Employees cried out for guidance, not silence, from a company too timid to accept education as its responsibility. How lucky were those who were prepped in advance for the inevitable economic downturn and exposure to the concept that those with a long time horizon—quite a ways from retirement—could be acquiring assets at bargain prices. Staying the course isn't easy if it has not been preached in advance.

If guidance is not available from the company or the outside experts it has retained, where do employees get it? CUNA Economics provides some answers in a December 28, 2016 position paper titled "Employees Dissatisfied With 401(k)s":

- 50 percent do not get help from providers and would like that opportunity.
- About one-third consult with family for help and suggestions while 41 percent of millennials do so.
- Some 88 percent know about company matches but a mere 24 percent understand related issues such as suggested contribution level or the sometimes-high fees associated with mutual funds.

Small business workers think their current provider does not inspire confidence concerning their future finances and find the plan difficult to understand.

Perhaps nowhere is ignorance as prevalent as in realization of the level of administrative costs and who pays.

BrightScope, a firm that rates the quality of company retirement plans, had this take on its website, brightscope.com:

> *What are the average fees in a 401(k) plan? I don't see any fees in my quarterly statement but my company has a poor score for "Total Plan Cost."*
>
> *Most 401(k) fees are netted against fund returns. What that means is that the investment return is reduced by the amount of the fee or cost. Thus, the gross return and the total economic impact to you of fees and costs are hidden. There are legislative and regulatory initiatives underway that would mandate full disclosure of all economic costs to your retirement plan account. Some combination of new legislation or enhanced regulatory disclosure requirement will likely resolve the lack of clarity surrounding 401(k) plans generally. Based on BrightScope data, the average 401(k) total plan cost can be as low as 0.20 percent for the largest plan and as high as 5 percent for smaller plans. Total plan cost is highly dependent upon the size of the plan, the average account balance of the plan and the type of provider used (bank, mutual fund company, insurance company, etc.). Total plan cost includes asset-based investment management fees, asset-based administrative and advice fees, and administration, and other fees including insurance charges. The conventional 401(k) statement does not itemize these fees, but simply shows reduced net returns so your account reconciles on your statement.*

There is or can be plenty of good news on the education front. Companies that have made the decision to offer a 401(k), or other financial benefits such as student loan repayment, have taken significant steps to ensure their workers' financial health.

Open Communication with Employees Is Key

Doesn't it make sense to inform employees to get the most out of what you're offering? Communicate regularly about the plan, inform employees about their options, and provide investment education so they can make the best decisions possible when it comes to planning for retirement.

401(k) Offers Opportunity

> *There's an enormous opportunity to educate people and make saving and investing feel approachable for the first time in a way that traditional financial services haven't been able to do. Companies have so many ways to communicate today, going beyond the traditional pamphlets or group PowerPoint presentations. Add social media and sharing of links to helpful financial websites. An independent advisor can do one-on-one meetings, getting across the basics in thirty minutes or so. Chances are what the participant really wants are answers to two or three specific questions.*

Plan sponsors should look for investment providers that offer financial and investment advice as part of their services, or they should find a trustworthy financial advisor (preferably one who is a fiduciary) who can conduct informational sessions for employees on a semi-regular basis. Employees won't fully appreciate the value of the benefits you're providing if they don't understand how they can maximize their investment.

In a previous chapter, the chief financial officer of a Northwest nonprofit said that, as she was preparing a retirement program, she was motivated as much as anything by the desire to change employee attitudes—especially those of millennials—toward saving and preparing for their futures. She felt that education needed to be much more than a packet passed out at new employee orientation. She felt her company should craft a consistent approach to disseminating information across with various methods.

We agree.

Summary

We've discussed the need and benefits of a great education program. Now we'll change up in the next chapter and have a little pop quiz. Are you ready?

CHAPTER SEVEN

How's Your Retirement Financial Knowledge?

Financial advisors often give new clients a short quiz—perhaps three to ten questions—to gauge their financial understanding on the most basic steps necessary to survive and prosper in retirement.

See how you can do on six questions culled from a master list of thirty-eight compiled by The American College in its 2017 retirement income literacy survey.

We'll print the six correct answers below. Be aware that even those who describe themselves as fairly knowledgeable about finances discover that the test is not that easy.

Pop Quiz

1. Sarah is single, age sixty-five, and takes a reverse mortgage with a lump sum payment. When does the loan have to be repaid?
When she permanently leaves the home
When she takes on any other loan
Whenever the mortgage company wants it back
When she attains age seventy
Don't know

2. Please choose the response below that best completes this statement: If you had a well-diversified portfolio of 50 percent stocks and 50 percent bonds that was worth $100,000 at retirement, based on historical returns in the U.S. the most you can afford to withdraw is ____ plus inflation each year to have a 95 percent chance that your assets will last for thirty years.
$2,000
$4,000
$6,000
$8,000
Don't know

3. Most experts agree that the best way to protect against inflation is to have:
A diversified portfolio of stocks
A diversified portfolio of bonds
A diversified portfolio of CDs (certificate of deposits)
Don't know

4. True or false? Exchange-traded funds generally have higher expenses than actively-managed mutual funds.
True
False

5. Which of the following types of long-term bonds typically has the highest yield?
AAA-rated corporate bonds
B-rated corporate bonds
Treasury bonds
Don't know

6. If 100 percent of a mutual fund's assets are invested in long-term bonds and the investment climate changes so that interest rates rise significantly, then the value of mutual fund shares:
Decrease significantly
May rise or fall depending upon the type of bond
Increase significantly
Will not change at all

Americans who are not financially literate typically find that a thirty-eight-question quiz is much longer than necessary to convince them of their shortcomings. The long quiz was developed through interviews with 1,019 Americans aged sixty to seventy-five, with at least a minimal level of household assets. It included questions on assets to maintain lifestyle, life expectancy, Social Security, early death of a spouse, annuities, taxes, and more.

So, what to do if you come up lacking in basic knowledge, short of taking a college class or hiring a wealth manager? Companies with sound 401(k) plans typically have an outside advisor involved who can come in to provide guidance/education through group seminars, videos, pamphlets or websites. Ask your company's HR department.

The thirty-eight-question quiz is available online at: https://retirement.theamericancollege.edu/retirement-101/retirement-income-literacy-quiz

A tip to those tempted to challenge the boss, the HR person, or the investment committee to take the quiz: Go ahead, just don't press them for how they did. It may not be career-enhancing.

Pop Quiz Answers

1. When does Sarah's reverse mortgage have to be repaid?
When she permanently leaves the home.

2. How much can be safely withdrawn each year from a well-diversified portfolio of $100,000?
$4,000.

3. What is the best way to protect your retirement portfolio against inflation?
Diversified portfolio of stocks. (Yes, advisors may suggest adding other asset classes besides stocks to reduce volatility, provide a steadier stream of income, or other reasons.)

4. True or false? Do exchange-traded funds (ETFs) generally have higher expenses than actively managed mutual funds?
False.

5. Which type of long-term bond typically has the highest yield?
B-rated corporate bonds.

6. If all a mutual fund's assets are invested in long-term bonds and interest rates in general rise significantly, what happens to the value of the mutual fund shares?
They decrease significantly.

Summary

How well did you do on the test? How well do you think your employees would do? If you didn't do as well as you thought you should have, that's the exact reason your 401(k) needs a great education program.

CHAPTER EIGHT

Three Rs of Retirement Plans: Rules, Risk, and Expert Relief

Forget Doris Day's signature song, "Que Sera, Sera" and the lyrics, "The future's not ours to see." Retirement plan sponsors can see a future packed full of change, if not certainty. Rather than "what will be, will be," plan administrators can take steps to ensure that their future goes in a positive direction.

This chapter is divided into three sections:
1. Wait, What If the Rules Change? (the threat of regulation)
2. Might I Get Sued? Prepare, Don't Panic (the threat of litigation)
3. Hire an Expert—You'll be Glad You Did (the prescribed solution)

The Department of Labor's 1,023-page new fiduciary rule, designed to relieve consumers of excessively high fees of $17 billion a year, by government estimate, was supposed to take effect June 9, 2017. Instructions on fully implementing the rule and enforcing it, however, were postponed to July 1, 2019 before a District Court of Appeal decision vacated the rule entirely . . . only to have the Department of Labor announce months later that it will be resurrecting portions of the rule to implement in the coming years. So, what to do in the light of constantly shifting goalposts?

Lawyers, becoming more familiar with plan abuses or flaws, have escalated the filing of lawsuits. Huge corporations are being pushed into financial settlements to avoid trials. Private universities, whose retirement plans evolved in a different way, today have repetitive layers of costly management and have been targeted. Relatively small retirement plans, modest in number of participants and assets under management, once were deemed not worth the trouble of suing and thus immune. A few cases have been filed recently, however, but still are presumed to be outliers.

The solution to regulatory uncertainty and the risk of litigation is to hire an expert. Several reasons are cited, including cost efficiencies in designing and running the plans and outsourcing much of the liability. The bottom line, simply stated, is: You have a business to run, so mind your business. Pass the details and the headaches onto an expert.

Wait, What If the Rules Change?

The rules governing retirement programs—401(k)s, traditional pensions and individual retirement accounts—really had not changed in forty years, not since the Employee Retirement Income Security Act (ERISA) was adopted in 1974. Change was overdue.

The Department of Labor's new rule, all 1,023 pages of it, was designed to expand ERISA provisions, not replace them. Because of lack of transparency, consumers generally are unaware of excessively high fees, conflicts of interest, and outright abuses. The government and consumer protection organizations are aware, however. Fees are too high—$17 billion a year too high—according to the White House Council of Economic Advisors in a 2015 report.

Years in the making, the initial Department of Labor's fiduciary rule was unveiled in April 2015. Powerful industry interests such as insurance companies and large brokerages feared loss of business, even being forced to drop out of this market. Companies large and small argued the rule was much too complex and that revisions and simplification were in order.

The final rule was approved in April 2016, only to collide with a new presidential administration intent on reducing, not adding, regulations. Indeed, President Donald Trump signed an executive order delaying implementation. The Department of Labor responded by adopting the rule effective June 9, 2017, but delaying administrative guidelines and enforcement until July 1, 2019.

A coalition of consumer groups, including Americans for Financial Reform and The American Federation of Labor and Congress of Industrial Organizations (AFL-CIO), called the delay "effectively a repeal of the fiduciary rule's most critical provisions." Finally, mid-2018 a court vacated the rule entirely . . . only for the Department of Labor to announce that it would resurrect portions of the rule for implementation down the road.

So, uncertainty abounds.

What is the gist of the fiduciary rule?

Advisors (the definition of advisor expanded to include any professional making a recommendation or solicitation) must put their clients' interests first, not just meet a lesser standard of suitability. They cannot conceal potential conflicts of interest and all fees and commissions must be disclosed in dollar amounts.

The fiduciary rule allows advisors to provide general investment guidance to clients, such as what asset classes may be appropriate based on their age and income.

The push for regulatory change already has caused ripples and even waves throughout the financial world. Companies are making internal changes. Consumers and plan sponsors' investment committees are becoming aware. Independent advisors who meet the fiduciary standard are saying, "Why wait for the inevitable? You can meet future regulations, better serve the needs of your employees, and enjoy lower costs immediately."

Change seems certain, even if certainty is nowhere to be seen.

One potential outcome is that heightened competition among players in the $7 trillion and growing 401(k) industry will help drive a shift to fiduciaries and putting clients' interests first instead of the lesser standard of whether the investmentproduct is suitable.

Debate Wages Over Fiduciary Rule

There will be winners and losers in the financial world with forced regulations or just the threat of possible forced regulatory changes.

The Fifth Circuit Court of Appeals ruled against the fiduciary standard in a 2-1 decision on March 15, 2018. On March 19, 2018 the U.S. Department of Labor announced that pending further review it would not enforce the fiduciary rule requiring all administrators of 401(k)s to meet fiduciary standards.

While the new rules were seen as impacting all financial advisors to some extent, it was expected that those who work on commission, such as brokers and insurance agents, would be affected the most.

Further, the Securities and Exchange Commission projected crafting its own set of fiduciary rules in April 2017 but a change in chairs has clouded the probability of change. The SEC conceivably could propose a broader rule covering even more financial products.

Increased compliance costs projected with adoption of the new rules already have forced some consolidation in the broker-dealer world. Unless partnering with larger players, small investment advisors might not have the financial resources to invest in the technology and the compliance expertise. Partnering clearly is in vogue. Even larger players have decided to leave the arena or are contemplating doing so. The brokerage operations of MetLife Inc. and American International Group were sold off in anticipation of these rules and the related costs.

Advisors and registered reps who only dabble in 401(k) plans might not find it profitable to continue. Annuity vendors, under threat of having to disclose their commissions to clients, could see significantly reduced sales.

It could be years before the legal system reaches a conclusion. In the meantime, players who already are fiduciaries say, "Why wait? Deal with us and we will put your interests first. You will have your bases covered."

The outcome could be shaped as well by consumer demand for transparency and company investment committees realizing, under the threat of litigation, that they can be liable for substandard plans poorly run.

Might I Get Sued? Prepare, Don't Panic

Lawsuits are on the rise, without question.

Consider that more than thirty cases were filed regarding excessive fees in retirement plans across the country in twelve months from late 2016-17. That compares with just eighty or so ERISA excessive-fee cases in the previous decade.[12]

Lawsuits can be scary, without question.

---

[12] Dilroop Sidhu, Groom Law Group, Chartered of Washington D.C. Plan Sponsor Council of America's newsletter, "Defined Contributions Insights," Fall 2017. https://www.psca.org/insights_fall_2017

They can come like a lightning bolt, out of a seemingly clear sky. If individuals are cited by name in the investment policy statement—say, the boss or the HR director—they can be found personally liable. The liability, attorneys say, cannot be discharged through bankruptcy. That is scary.

Litigation is a distraction that business executives don't need. Retired attorney and newspaper executive Harold Fuson of San Diego was fond of saying at seminars: "Even if the lawsuits are without merit, they are a worry. They destroy brain cells."

But let's put this fright into perspective. Thirty lawsuits may seem like a lot but there were 533,769 of these 401(k) plans in existence at the end of 2014, plus another 107,000 of other types.[13] The point is to prepare—not panic—and to avoid being discouraged from starting or improving a retirement plan that employees covet, and even expect.

There are best practices that, with documentation, can act to negate an allegation that your company acted imprudently. While the plan sponsor always has the ultimate responsibility of supervising administration of a plan, it can pass off considerable liability to a qualified expert hired as a co-fiduciary.

Three types of excessive-fee cases predominate, continues Sidhu in the "Defined Contributions Insights" newsletter referenced above.

The first are lawsuits against large corporate plan sponsors challenging fees and expenses. The cases allege that sponsors breached their ERISA fiduciary duties by selecting investment options that are overly expensive, underperforming, or imprudent when compared to alternative options. The large companies are pressured to settle with attorneys collecting a third or more. How

---

[13] Department of Labor, Abstract of 2014 Form 5500 Annual Reports.
https://www.dol.gov/agencies/ebsa/researchers/statistics/retirement-bulletins/private-pension-plan

large are the companies? Think American Airlines ($22 million settlement) and Boeing Company ($57 million).

The second type involves financial institutions who also happen to be plan sponsors. These cases make similar claims as in the first type, but also allege that these plan sponsors used affiliated investment products and service providers to increase the financial institution's revenue. Think New York Life Insurance Company ($3 million settlement), Merrill Lynch ($25 million), or Massachusetts Mutual Life Insurance Company ($30.9 million).

The third type has recently been initiated against private university-sponsored 403(b) plans. These plans developed under a different system than the modern 401(k)s and often overlap. The allegation is that fiduciary responsibility is breached by offering large, complex investment lineups with options that are expensive, duplicative, and poorly performing.

Small businesses, not to feel neglected, have been targeted in a few cases filed recently. The allegations are similar, only the modest size is new. Think *Damberg v. LaMettry's Collision, Inc.* ($9 million in assets, 114 participants and voluntarily dismissed by plaintiffs on June 17, 2016), *Bernaola v. Checksmart Financial* ($25 million in assets and 1,700 participants, filed July 14, 2016 and pending), and *Schmitt v. Nationwide Insurance Co.* ($1 million in assets and twenty-seven participants, filed June 27, 2017 and pending).

If a lawsuit is a lightning bolt, several key cases suggest plenty of rays of sunshine are breaking through the clouds, concludes Sidhu. *White v. Chevron* was dismissed—twice. *Brotherston v. Putnam Investments, LLC* was decided in Putnam's favor and indicates cases against financial institutions are proving increasingly difficult for plaintiffs to win. There is hope for university plan sponsors, too, as the University of Pennsylvania successfully had *Sweda vs. University of Pennsylvania* dismissed.

The odds of having a lawsuit merely filed against a plan—30 in 533,769—are lottery-style slim. Still, there are ways to make the odds even better with prudent business practices. That brings us to section three.

Hire an Expert—You'll be Glad You Did

Law firm partner Todd Solomon of McDermott Will & Emery LLP in Washington, D.C. presented at a seminar of employee benefit specialists in Denver on September 19, 2017. Solomon spoke to the International Society of Certified Employee Benefit Specialists about the responsibilities of plan fiduciaries.

Responsibilities include:

- Acting solely in the interest of plan participants and their beneficiaries
- Carrying out their duties prudently
- Following the plan documents
- Diversifying plan investments
- Paying only reasonable expenses

The bottom line is that avoiding fiduciary liability requires that a fiduciary engage in a prudent and deliberative decision-making process and document the process thoroughly. Fiduciaries are judged according to the procedural process they undertake.

Solomon restated his points on the lessons to be learned from the litigation of recent years:

- Meet regularly and document the process.
- Address underperforming funds quickly.
- Adopt an investment policy statement and follow it.

- Review vendors periodically and conduct a request for proposals (RFP) for lower fees.
- Engage a qualified, independent advisor and pay reasonable fees.
- Consider elimination of revenue sharing.
- Make sure you are in the lowest fee (mutual fund) share class.

Aside from changing regulations and litigation possibilities, there are plenty of reasons to consider hiring an independent advisor and outsourcing functions. The boss of a mid-size firm, say, one hundred to five hundred employees, may have been the founder, building it up from almost nothing. Yet he or she undoubtedly has had little or no exposure or training in running employee retirement programs. Most likely, neither do those who sit on the investment committee, not even the HR director.

Worse, investment committee members have jam-packed schedules and their "day jobs" need tending to. Another meeting to talk about 401(k) issues is time spent away from what they are supposed to be doing. Many employees are lost without some guidance on investing in general and how to get the most out of the retirement plan. Does any committee member want to lead the informational sessions?

Anybody?

A 401(k) Plan Is Not Do-It-Yourself

It's worth stating again: You're an expert in your business. So, mind your business. Bring in an independent advisor who is an expert on many of the things you are not.

Best Practices for Plan Sponsors[14]

• **Duty to Monitor:** Rigorously monitor and periodically reassess investment management and recordkeeping fees to ensure they are reasonable.

• **Document the Process:** Follow sound governance procedures and have a well-documented process for making fiduciary decisions. Keep written minutes and Investment Policy Statements to show how the fiduciaries involved (plan sponsor and hired experts) consider quality service and price when selecting or monitoring investment options.

• **Use Advisors:** Understand the advice, and ask questions, of qualified, independent advisors.

Summary

In this chapter we discussed the rules, the risks, the confusing regulations, and the recommendation that you hire a fiduciary advisor to help navigate the changing landscape. Next chapter I will give you a look behind the scenes at the power of a great custodian supporting a great fiduciary.

---

[14] Todd Solomon. Partner of McDermott Will & Emery LLP of Chicago. Solomon's presentation at 36th annual symposium of International Society of Certified Employee Specialists, September 19, 2017, in Denver, Colorado.

CHAPTER NINE

An Invisible Army Is Behind Each Independent Advisor

There are a lot of moving parts and pieces to a great 401(k). We've stressed the need for a fiduciary advisor. But what does a fiduciary advisor need to be successful?

The Registered Investment Advisor who pitches a company on handling its retirement plan is backed by an army—an invisible army.

The independent advisor, in the rapidly emerging retirement plan model, is typically supported by a large firm that handles the money transactions and recordkeeping. The custodian firm is present but rarely seen. It has little or no direct contact with either the plan sponsor or the participants (employees) involved in the retirement program.

The independent advisor model gaining market share is built on a well-defined division of labor backed by the resources the custodian firm provides behind the scenes.

How does the system work from the perspective of the unseen army?

Of the many qualified custodians, we turned to TD Ameritrade (TDA). Well known for its 100-plus retail brokerage locations in the United States, TD Ameritrade and its 10,400 employees also serve as a custodian for more than 5,700 Registered Investment Advisors (at year-end 2017).

We interviewed two of those 10,400 TDA employees. Kristin Cogar manages the playbook, the vast array of informational services and support the firm provides to independent advisors. Michael Lyons is involved in inside sales, meaning he is involved as a point of contact—but stationed at a central location—as the advisors recruit corporate clients, design plans to better serve their needs at lower cost, and inform their employee participants.

We interviewed Cogar and Lyons. Here are their stories.

KRISTIN COGAR
Senior Product Specialist
TD Ameritrade Corporate Retirement Plan Solutions

Q. Do you work primarily with people such as registered investment advisors who help companies [plan sponsors] come up with retirement programs for management and employees?

A. The TD Ameritrade Retirement Plan solution was created to support independent Registered Investment Advisors who wanted to service the plan sponsor clients. It is built to satisfy the high expectations of advisors, plan sponsors, and participants alike with a combination of broad investment selection, outstanding service, robust tools, and the comfort and stability that come with the TD Ameritrade brand. Since we don't sell direct to plan sponsors, I have limited contact, if any, with plan sponsors and participants.

Q. Please explain what Corporate Retirement Plan Solutions is.

A. Corporate Retirement Plans Solutions is a term that encompasses TD Ameritrade's product offering for businesses that offer their employees a retirement plan.

Q. Using a football analogy, some say you manage the playbook. What is the investment playbook that you manage?

A. The playbook is a website that contains tools and resources to help Registered Investment Advisors guide their entry or expansion into the retirement plan market. It provides strategy, tactics, and advice from industry experts. The retirement plan market is complex, but for an independent Registered Investment Advisors, one differentiator can be the fiduciary status that they take on as either an investment advisor or investment manager of the plan and being able to help plan sponsors meet and understand their own fiduciary requirements.

Q. So TDA may help advisors with a host of services such as crafting a menu of investment options, record keeping, tax reporting, monitoring of new regulations, and providing materials for the education of sponsors and participants. Let's look at the services you offer, working of course with other TDA employees to help the independent advisors.

A. We service a range of plan types, including 401(k) and 403(b) plans, 457 plans, and non-qualified defined contribution plans.

Our comprehensive services and support make it easy for advisors, plan sponsors, and participants.

For plan sponsors:

- Full-service recordkeeping, plan administration, and custodial services

- Plan design support

- Participant enrollment support and materials

- Plan documents and supporting forms

- Compliance testing

- Form 5500 preparation

- Guaranteed timely payment of mutual fund revenue sharing

- Directed trustee services may be available

- Easy access to plan information online or by phone

- Rollover assistance when participants leave the plan

- Downloadable reports

- Auto enrollment and auto increase programs

- Dedicated relationship support

- Plan sponsor-focused website with streamlined payroll administration, participant enrollment, and reporting

For participants:

• A comprehensive website with thoughtfully selected resources for account management and more

• Twenty-four-hour access to customer service and support

• Online enrollment, with related support and materials

• Daily valuation of accounts

• Personalized rates of return/performance

• Data exports

• Rebalancing capabilities

• Online educational support, including digital retirement planning tools

• A robust resource center

• Investment information

• Rollover assistance when leaving the plan

For advisors:

• A dedicated sales force

• Easy access to an experienced, knowledgeable support team

• A playbook with advisor tools to help them build their business, sell and service retirement plans

- Extensive materials, including tools, a comprehensive plan proposal, and educational opportunities

- An open-architecture investment framework that provides them with great flexibility to create and monitor their clients' investment menus

Q. The praise that advisors have for you would probably make you blush. Any gaps in their knowledge that you help fill in?

A. Very kind words, thank you! We continue to see opportunities to help advisors find prospecting and business growth tools and strategies. In addition to the resources we have on the playbook for RIAs to use, TD Ameritrade also has regional events for advisors. These events allow advisors to interact with each other and share experiences, especially success stories.

Q. Let's talk about FinTech—sophisticated software—and the amazing way possible choices for an investment portfolio can be analyzed in a heartbeat.

A. TD Ameritrade offers advisors a retirement investment platform with a true open architecture. This provides the freedom and flexibility advisors need to choose the best solutions for each plan sponsor. From a universe of mutual funds, exchange-traded funds and self-directed brokerage accounts from our brokerage affiliate to collective investment funds, unitized managed accounts, stable value funds, employer stock, and more. They have access to a wide variety of products across many different styles.

All the independent advisors on our platform have very different investment strategies for their personal wealth business, separate from the retirement plans they handle. Our platform allows them to use the same investment strategies for both. With unitized managed accounts [UMAs], advisors can deliver a managed, customized investment strategy with full-fee disclosure at a competitive price. UMAs are advisor-managed portfolios that are valued or "unitized" daily and may include publicly traded equities, privately held stocks, ETFs, and mutual funds.

Q. Can you share a couple human interest vignettes where you have had a satisfying experience making a real difference for a group of people?

A. I really enjoy what I do and being able to hear—the vast majority of my interactions are over the phone—the "aha moment." That happens when an advisor sees the value he or she can provide to a plan sponsor, and the company executive comes to understand that they don't have to be the expert on everything about retirement plans. After all, that's what we are here for and why we provide the resources we do on the playbook. I've talked to many advisors who are unsure if they want to get involved in retirement plans because they believe it is too complicated and they are struggling with how to take the conversation that they are comfortable with—talking to a wealth management client—to discussions with plan sponsors, and eventually, speaking to participants in a group setting. These audiences are different, and how you engage with them will change dramatically. Recently I helped a Registered Investment Advisor firm with participant enrollment meetings for a company with multiple locations. The discussions we had when talking about using any technology available and modifying the conversation by understanding what participants really want to hear was very satisfying for me.

Q. Kristin, any final thoughts?

A. I am very fortunate to work for a company which believes in and advocates for the registered investment advisor model. TD Ameritrade's platform really is designed to be a platform and not the entire solution. We rely on the Registered Investment Advisor for the investment strategy and approach, which allows each advisor to bring an entirely different solution, a different flavor to the table.

The advisors can help plan sponsors understand and meet their fiduciary responsibilities. In my experience, most companies don't understand that as plan sponsors they are acting in the role of plan fiduciary, or what that even means. Advisors who can communicate and help plan sponsors meet their requirements are able to differentiate themselves from other advisors and become a trusted partner to the company.

MICHAEL LYONS
Retirement Plan Sales Consultant
TD Ameritrade

Q. Do you do what is called inside sales, and what does that entail?

A. Yes, my role is internal sales consultant for our Retirement Plan Solutions (RPS) sales team. We support 401(k) plans and a few other types of corporate group retirement programs. I don't work directly with plan participants. Instead, in my role I am often the first retirement contact for advisors. I make myself available via phone or email to answer any initial questions. As I am the first line of support for advisors, I often work with them to find the right retirement product or solution for various sizes and types of plans. For newer advisors, I help explain why they should consider building a retirement practice and what key things they will need to consider. For more seasoned advisors, I assist in building proposals and running plan analyses to help win more business. For plan sponsors, I help educate them about how TD Ameritrade works with their advisors and explain how our services, tools and materials can help support them.

Q. How does inside sales differ from outside sales?

A. My role is primarily to support advisors via the phone, or WebEx remotely, whereas my external colleagues travel to meet with advisors and sponsors face to face. We work as a team to support advisors and help them succeed in this space.

Q. Can you provide a sense of TD Ameritrade service levels?

A. With the TD Ameritrade Retirement Plan, we bundle the TPA [third-party administrator], recordkeeping, and custodial services under one contract and one fee schedule. We provide a dedicated relationship manager to assist advisors and sponsors with any plan-related service needs.

This is a unique service approach, as many other providers will only assign a dedicated support person if the plan is very large. Additionally, TD Ameritrade provides a call center to help answer participants' questions.

Q. As I understand it, TD Ameritrade does not have any proprietary products, meaning they have nothing to gain whether Product A or Product B is chosen?

A. Correct. Accordingly, TD Ameritrade Trust has a true open architecture framework to provide an impressive range of investment solutions. We currently provide access to more than 13,000 mutual funds and 1,100 ETFs, advisor-managed unitized managed accounts [UMAs], collective investment funds [CIFs] and self-directed brokerage accounts [SDBAs]. So, we offer real choice. Advisors can mix and match and choose investments that fit their investment strategy.

Q. How different is this approach of independent advisors teaming with custodians than one of, say, dealing with insurance companies?

A. In the past, if advisors wanted to have an easy way to set up a retirement plan they traditionally used an insurance platform or DCIO fund company, because they offered a bundled product. [DCIO stands for defined contribution investment only. In this case it refers to the platforms of a nonaffiliated recordkeeper.] The potential downside to this approach was that advisors were often forced to use proprietary products or choose from limited and expensive investment options that paid the retirement plan platform a share of the revenue.

TD Ameritrade Institutional has been in the business of helping advisors for a long time, and our retirement platform was designed with them in mind from the beginning. Our platform combines the streamlined services for the plan while preserving the investment flexibility and choice for the advisors.

Q. What are the potential advantages to the plan sponsor?

A. In our 2015 Plan Sponsor Sentiment Survey, plan sponsors told us that they agree that Registered Investment Advisors are better at providing value-added services such as education and retirement plan support than competing brokerage firms, investment firms and retirement plan consultants. Sponsors benefit by having a fiduciary advisor able to select and choose potentially lower cost investments with straightforward transparent pricing for administrative services.

Advisors are free to do their jobs as fiduciaries while letting our team of experienced professionals provide reliable recordkeeping and plan administrative services.

Q. Who is doing the recordkeeping and tax reporting in this arrangement?

A. By contract, TD Ameritrade Trust is responsible for all recordkeeping, TPA administration, tax reporting and plan design. This is true for any plan using our bundled retirement plan product.

Q. There are no guarantees or promises on investment results, of course. Do you have a standard answer on how much, say, a sixty-basis-point reduction in annual fees compounded over X years means?

A. Each plan and situation is unique, but the effect of lowered fees over time does have a huge compounding effect. We offer advisors several different tools to help compare total plan costs and fees and explain these to the plan sponsors. Some plan sponsors think their plans are free because they are not paying any out-of-pocket costs. Our tools enable advisors to look at the total cost to the plan from investments, wrap fees, and direct provider expenses. They can then compare a current plan's cost to what a new plan might look like.

Q. Are some company owners waking up to the fact that administrative costs are important because they, too, are participants and likely paying fees on much higher contribution amounts?

A. Many of our advisors point this out to their plan sponsor clients. In addition, we see plan sponsors asking for more assistance with understanding their fiduciary responsibilities. Advisors are well-positioned to help them in this regard.

Q. With the Department of Labor's push for a fiduciary rule and other changes, do you see the independent advisors and cooperating custodians poised to take advantage of this?

A. Registered Investment Advisors are already working as fiduciaries, so they may be better suited to take advantage of the coming rule changes than other insurance reps or broker/dealers.

Q. Mike, any final thoughts?

A. Our role is to help advisors and sponsors better understand the retirement market and how to be successful. Advisors do not have to be retirement experts in every respect as we have many tenured associates with vast knowledge and experience who can provide the advisor with retirement plan bench strength.

Summary

Everyone should play to their strengths. You are best at managing your business or running your department, so do that, and relegate being a custodian to an organization like TD Ameritrade and being a 401(k) fiduciary advisor to someone like me.

CHAPTER TEN

Doing an RFP—
Be Careful What You Ask For

What is an RFP? An RFP is a "request for proposal." If you're looking to establish a new 401(k) or want to explore options to move your 401(k) plan to a fiduciary, you ask advisors to submit their offer, or competitive bid.

Before you commit to receiving one or more RFPs, you want to assess your current plan. First, score your plan (www.401k-Score.com). Second, benchmark your plan (www.401k-Benchmark.com). After receiving your score and benchmark, you may want to take the next step of RFPs.

Knowing when to do a search, or request for proposals, for a potential new retirement plan advisor is easy—every four to five years is the short answer according to the conventional wisdom. Regulations, market forces and competitive pricing can change rapidly. Why continue to pay Cadillac-level fees if prices have dropped substantially since the last time you hired outside help? If new features are available, ones your current advisor and custodian perhaps do not offer, you probably will be in the dark unless you do a search.

Knowing when to do a search may come even sooner if employee complaints are piling up at HR and it is apparent your current program is not working well.

Doing comparison shopping every so often is a prudent business practice and the RFP is the means of accomplishing that with retirement plan vendors.

How to Save Yourself Time and Trouble

Knowing how to craft the request document is not easy. Seeking out too many potential bidders is a sure way to bury your investment committee members and keep them from performing their real jobs. Vendors do not appreciate cattle calls where they are required to do onerous preparation work with little chance of winning new business.

Send out a request document that contains muddled questions or fails to ask about what is most important to your company and surely you will wind up with a mountain of responses that cannot be compared with each other. If the vendors don't understand the question, how can they give you a clear answer?

There is a quick, easy way to find an expert—you could just grab the Kevin you play golf with and who is sort of in the industry, or the friend from your college days who works for a company a couple of states away. They will be only too willing to handle your firm's account. Alas, many an entrepreneur has discovered that when a major problem occurs, the friend has neither the expertise nor the resources available to solve the issue.

There are several resource organizations with model questions, material, and even RFP templates to offer to guide your search. Just three are 401khelpcenter.com, fi360.com, and Retirement Advisor Council.

Speaking of RFP templates, I prefer mine. It gets the job done, it stays on topic, and it doesn't drown you in information you don't have the time or inclination to process. (Is it crucial to know how many clients a vendor added last year, how many he lost, and why? Do you really expect to get candid answers as to why from all twelve responding bidders?)

Let's examine the big picture before we plunge in.

There are three types of delivery systems where vendors can provide your firm with retirement program services:

• ***Bundled.*** Everything comes in one convenient package that is designed primarily for small firms. Keep it simple, keep the cost from becoming prohibitive as small firms lack economy of scale, and no changes are permitted. This is the financial world's version of the restaurant menu that says, "No substitutions allowed."

• **Unbundled.** One vendor will provide your firm with everything. Yes, you can mix and match. The danger is the unseen log floating just below the surface as your speedboat zooms across the lake. Are you buying the vendor's own products, ones that are more expensive? Are you blocked from having a much better version because the vendor does not want to sell a competitor's product? Examples of unbundled providers are insurance companies and mega-brokerages.

• **Alliance.** This system is rapidly gaining market share and is a focus of this book. Well-trained and credentialed independents can step in, design, and oversee the retirement program, either on a suggest-and-gain approval (a 3(21) advisor), or on an almost-full-discretion basis (a 3(38) advisor). These independents turn to someone else, often a large brokerage firm, to do the recordkeeping and handle the financial transactions. The system can provide specialized expertise up front and can eliminate some of the problems inherent in staying under just one umbrella. Nationally branded stock brokerages welcome the trend and are actively promoting the concept.

There are several major steps to sending out an RFP.

First comes some internal soul-searching. (Why are we doing this now and what don't we like about our current program?)

Second are the qualifications we think we want in an advisor and whether we can be flexible on a particular point so as to not rule out an otherwise outstanding candidate.

Third are such nitty-gritty mechanics such as how and where to respond, deadlines, and when a decision will be rendered.

Fourth is the questionnaire itself. Companies are well-advised to use and modify a template. I'm partial to my own template. If you'd like a copy, call my office at 206-362-0503.

Fifth is the challenge of finding potential candidates, the reasonable number of responses you are prepared to handle, and making the parameters clear so vendors are treated fairly and you receive answers and pricing that can be compared.

Soul-Searching

The vendor needs to know what is most important to you and is lacking in your current program. If you haven't pinpointed that, how can he? Are there too many employee complaints? Is the cost too high? Is education almost nonexistent? Is the program taking up too much staff time?

Qualifications

Does the vendor have specialized knowledge? Experience? Is he or she a fiduciary, and what kind—comfortable with waiting until suggestions are finally approved, or prefers to have the discretion to submit recommendations and immediately go ahead?

The vendor's support system is very important to having a smooth relationship. Who will be doing the recordkeeping and handling the money? If employees have questions, whom do they call—HR, the advisor, or his support team? Is there a call center, and is it nearby or several time zones away? Is it staffed in the United States or outsourced to who knows where? Will it be available to employees on their schedules or will it close long before they get off work? What kind of software is the vendor using to build a menu of investment choices and to monitor the results? Can he or she teach employees very basic investing concepts—in English, instead of jargon?

Be sure to build some flexibility into the qualifications, just as you would in recruiting an executive. Some prerequisite might be desirable but not necessary. Why discourage someone, perhaps a top candidate, from even applying?

The Mechanics

The vendors need to be well-informed about the process. Do you want the responses electronically or on paper? How many copies and where should they be sent? How do you want the fees broken down and listed so that there can be a clear comparison?

Internally, you need to have some understanding in advance about how you will whittle down the field. How can you avoid spending an inordinate amount of time on someone who will not make the cut? Okay, you hire employees all the time; maybe this aspect isn't that hard. Or maybe it is because few hires make a substantial difference in the financial well-being of your employees and you.

Questionnaire

Before potential candidates can even answer the questions, they need to know about your company and your screening process. How many employees are currently working for you? What is the pay scale? What is the average level of education and typical age of the workers? Who is a contact person who can answer further questions?

Vendors need to know what you want before they can supply it. Provide a copy of the current program and where it comes up short, in your view. Describe the various features of the package you want. Are you looking for education using several types of media? More-detailed or less-detailed employee statements? Are you open to automatic enrollment and automatic raise? Is self-directed investing something you would like to have available for sophisticated employees?

Is it Time to Get Competitive Bids?

An Efficient Way

Once you've scored (www.401k-Score.com) and benchmarked (www.401k-Benchmark.com) your 401(k), you will know if it's time to look for a plan that meets your exact needs.

There's a lot to consider. The "easy" way out is to use a comprehensive, boilerplate document with tons of pages. That's not the best use of your time.

Decide what you want from your 401(k) plan. Is your ideal plan bare bones and do it yourself? Or is your ideal plan fiduciary advised, supported by best practices and modern fintech?

Once you've decided, visit www.401kRescueExperts.com to use my guidelines. Research shows that plan sponsors want:

- A diversified, high scoring, low fee, investment lineup

- A comprehensive education plan for themselves and their employees, taught by an instructor with real experience

- A fiduciary advisor who puts the 401(k)'s needs before their own

These are the critical issues, and my advice is to focus on them in your request for proposal.

Summary: Best practices and due diligence call for getting competitive RFPs every four or five years.

Finding Candidates

You can certainly ask others for referrals, especially similar-sized firms that have recently made a change. You might have a file with potential candidates who have made cold calls over the years.

Requesting multiple RFPs might be too burdensome for some, but my advice is to do your due diligence to the best of your ability if you're looking to really be an ally for your employees.

The quantity of questions is less important than the quality—the few that are key to your operation. The questions you do ask should be tough questions. If the answers are evasive, follow-up questions should very direct.

Is It Time to Get Competitive Bids?

An Efficient Way

Once you've scored (www.401k-Score.com) and benchmarked (www.401k-Benchmark.com) your 401(k), you will know if it's time to look for a plan that meets your exact needs.

There's a lot to consider. The "easy" way out is to use a comprehensive, boilerplate document with tons of pages. That's not the best use of your time.

Decide what you want from your 401(k) plan. Is your ideal plan bare bones and do-it-yourself (and accepting full regulatory responsibility for your actions)? Or is your ideal plan fiduciary advised, supported by best practices and modern FinTech?

Here is what the research shows that plan sponsors want:
- A diversified, high scoring, low fee, investment lineup
- A comprehensive education plan for themselves and their employees, taught by an instructor with real experience
- A fiduciary advisor, who puts the 401(k)'s needs before their own

These are the critical issues, and my advice is to focus on them in your request for proposal.

Summary

Best practices and due diligence call for getting competitive RFPs every four or five years.

CHAPTER ELEVEN

How Two Companies Switched Advisors

It may seem like a daunting undertaking to find and change financial advisors for your entire company. However, a plan sponsor has the fiduciary obligation to take care of the people using its plan. So, to "help the medicine go down," it may be useful to draw on the experience of other companies and see how others have handled this task. Following are the accounts of two different companies with different workforces and industries.

Pacific Rehabilitation Centers

"We gained cost savings, flexibility, and more."

Pacific Rehabilitation Centers is a company that made the switch—and the staff members are glad they did.

Formerly known as United Backcare, it is a firm of sixty employees that provides physical and psychological rehabilitation services at three locations in the state of Washington. The staff consists of highly trained professionals—physicians, psychologists, occupational therapists, vocational therapists, physical therapists and nurses—along with the support personnel—intake, insurance verification, human resources, accounting, receptionists, and C-suite executives.

Pacific Rehabilitation had its previous retirement program with an insurance company. The broker handling the financial transactions was not a fiduciary. Pacific Rehabilitation switched. The new arrangement is with an independent investment advisor—a certified fiduciary—and a national brokerage company (also a fiduciary) to handle the money transactions and several support services formerly done in-house. With sixty employees, the HR department previously was kept very busy with the recordkeeping workload alone.

With the new system in place for almost a year, it was a convenient point to take stock. What were the factors in making the switch? How does the new system work? Are they happy?

There are two easy ways to take stock. One way is by talking to the chief executive officer, a cheerful, enthusiastic woman, and a positive role model for professionals helping clients overcome very serious injuries. A busy CEO gets the big picture while avoiding getting bogged down in the details.

Another way to take stock is a document that the head of human resources, with assistance from the new advisor, prepared to acquaint employees with the new program and a candid appraisal of the costs. In short, here are the details.

Meet Regine Neiders, Ph.D., owner, CEO, and thirty-year veteran with the company. She was educated at the University of Washington and her work history includes a year at a hospital and seven years at a medical center before coming to Pacific Rehabilitation Centers. Following is an interview with her about the company's 401(k) journey.

Q. How did you find your new advisor?

A. I met the advisor during a three-evening retirement planning class. I was very impressed by his knowledge and approach and asked for a written proposal as well as a face-to-face follow-up presentation.

Q. What were the factors important to you in making the switch? Previously, you were with an insurance company and broker, who was not a fiduciary.

A. Yes. The most important factors were flexibility as well as cost reduction, plus time reduction for our HR staff. There were some cost savings which will compound with time. There are various kinds of services available to us that we did not have before. The advisor offers financial consulting and classes for the staff. I have consulted with him at the worksite and over the phone. His suggestions have been successful. He already has met with most of the staff.

Q. Are you satisfied with the new arrangement?

A. Very. The advisor has provided more value in respect to informing us about our options.

Q. Technically, your retirement program is now a 404(c) plan. Why
is that?

A. We have added a self-directed option, enabling the employees to make other choices. We have provided them material that explains the responsibilities and the cost.

Q. Under the new system the advisor came up with the menu of choices and educates the staff. The brokerage handles the money and recordkeeping. Were there other services or functions offloaded?

A. Yes. Previously we had to do a lot of calculating. Of course, we still transmit the payroll data to the broker. Our staff is very grateful to be relieved of much of the burden.

Q. You mentioned cost savings?

A. The administrative cost savings start at $3,000 a year for the company. The pool of participating employees gained a reduction in fees of $9,000 per year that can be used for investing. I'd refer you to HR or the advisor for further details.

Q. That is money that goes into employee investment choices and compounds tax-sheltered over time instead of being eaten up by administrative costs?

A. (laughs) You do understand. Correct.

The other way of taking stock is a ten-page document in plain English supplied to employees to introduce the new plan. The document opens bluntly, sharing the Great Secret most American workers do not know:

> "What fees do I pay when participating?" For many participants, that question may come as a surprise. There's an assumption that the answer is "None."
>
> In fact, there are costs associated with your participation in the plan. Participants pay for the cost of the plan's administration. There are also other costs that plan participants pay. And those expenses have an impact on the size of your account balance at retirement.

Many firms provide a matching contribution as an incentive to encourage employees to participate in the retirement savings program. Because companies may provide matching contributions, employees assume their employer pays administrative costs as well. That assumption is false.

The Pacific Rehabilitation document given to employees explains that the costs are deducted based on the value of plan assets. In the breakdown of costs for Pacific Rehabilitation, .55 percent goes for administrative costs, .75 percent for the investment advisor for a total of 1.30 percent a year. Both percentages are based upon the value of plan assets each year.

The document goes on to list the choices on the menu (self-directed participants can add more). One section provides performance results for the past one, three, and five years compared to benchmarks over the same periods.

The other section provides the annual operating expense for each menu item.

The sixty employees at Pacific Rehabilitation have the investment world at their fingertips.

There are eleven stock choices, five bond selections, eight blended options and two cash/stable value vehicles. In this case, the investment advisor came up with the menu choices, guided by sophisticated financial software evaluating the possible universe according to twelve criteria he deemed most relevant.

The fiduciary brokerage involved has no proprietary products and accordingly nothing of its own to peddle for the list.

You want a pool of large company stocks? That's on the list. So are small companies, foreign companies, growth companies, value companies, and health and technology sectors. What's more, there are index funds for those who prefer passive investments.

The blended category is for those who would like to have their retirement portfolios on autopilot. The eight-target retirement-date funds by Vanguard automatically reduce the risk as the participant ages and gets closer to retirement.

Vanguard made the final cut for the target-date funds. No company, however, dominates the list of choices. You'll find familiar names such as Fidelity, PowerShares, Principal, Prudential, and more.

The document concludes with a sage warning:

> The cumulative effect of fees and expenses can substantially reduce the growth of your retirement savings . . . Fees and statistics are only two of many factors to consider when you decide to invest in an option. You may also want to think about whether an investment in a particular option, along with your other investments, will help you achieve your financial goals.

How true. Statistical tables guide, but are not a substitute for, human oversight.

A 300-Employee Nonprofit

"We're a different company now. We've grown."

It is not difficult to conduct a search for firms to handle your company's retirement plan and to compare their proposals against the current arrangement. With market changes, new Department of Labor rules, and fiduciary responsibilities to employees to keep costs low, it is prudent to do so.

In a candid interview, one chief financial officer described how her firm handled the search and the selection of companies for a new and more effective arrangement. We have paired that interview with the detailed cost analysis of present and proposed plans submitted by one of the three finalists seeking to win the contract.

The CFO asked that she and her firm not be identified by name. She is an industry veteran and worked for other companies before assuming her current position. The company is a nonprofit with about 300 employees working at various sites in the state of Washington.

The retirement plan—nonprofit versions of the 401(k) are known as 403(b)—had been handled for a long time by a major insurance company and a small financial broker as custodian. During that time the demand for the nonprofit's services had soared. So had its employee count and the amount of retirement contributions under management.

The nonprofit provides a partial match for up to 5 percent of an employee's contributions after one year of service. About 80 percent of the employees participate.

Q. How did you decide to send out your request for proposals?

A. We decided against doing a general call. Instead, we sent invitations to six potential firms. These were based on recommendations, occasional sales calls over the years, and associations with previous employers. We specified what criteria were most important to us.

The second step was to evaluate the responses and select three finalist advisors for face-to-face interviews with myself and the retirement plan committee.

Q. Why did you decide to do a search in early 2017?

A. There were several reasons for the timing. I believe it is a sound business practice to do a review every so often, probably every five years. We had been with the current team—an insurance company and small broker—for a long, long time.

In a sense, we're a different company now. We've grown. We have gone from a small plan to one with more than $5 million of contributions under management.

The outside firms involved had changed as well. With the DOL [Department of Labor] rule changes involving fiduciaries, the insurance company wanted to withdraw from a co-fiduciary role. The broker was getting close to retiring. It seemed like an optimal time.

Q. So you selected a new team. Presumably it is too early to issue them a report card?

A. Yes, the switch is effective January 1, 2018.

Q. What were some of the criteria you listed as important to you?

A. We wanted more than handling of a retirement plan, we wanted an approach inclusive for all retirement aspects. I can explain that in a bit. We wanted an up-to-date training and education program. We wanted a new way of doing things instead of the same old, same old.

Q. Were there some administrative cost savings in switching?

A. Yes, there were some.

Q. Were employees concerned about administrative costs?

A. I don't think employees—especially new employees—know that much about administrative costs. They are overwhelmed with information overload in the hiring or coming-on-board process. I'm not aware of employee complaints.

Q. How about reducing the workload on the HR department?

A. HR still must coordinate.

Q. I'm getting the sense that the switch was about more than dollars and cents for you?

A. We want to change employee attitudes about saving and retirement planning. It is not just about the retirement plan, it is about Social Security, personal savings, considering long-term care, preparing for a new life stage.

We have a diverse staff, many young and some close to retirement. Especially with the newest generation of employees, we need to instill in them the importance of saving for the retirement years.

Q. Is participation voluntary? What is the level of participation?

A. About 80 percent. Participation was voluntary until about two years ago. We adopted an automatic default-in approach. New hires are enrolled at a 1 percent participation level.

Q. That still leaves free money—some company match—on the table.

A. Yes it does. We are considering an automatic escalation [where the default contribution would rise over time, perhaps linked to future pay raises].

Q. What forms will the employee education take?

A. All of them—pamphlets, seminars, face to face, online links. It will be multiple points of contact, not just at hiring and orientation. We must find a consistent way of getting their attention. Preparing for retirement is that important, even for the very young.

Q. Too early for a report card but you must have a feeling of confidence in your choice?

A. My opinion is the new approach will set well with the new generation of employees starting out; that they will take to heart the need to save for retirement.

The Great Secret that the American workforce does not know is who pays the administrative costs for 401(k) plans. Under traditional pension programs, the employer pays for everything. Not so for 401(k) programs, rare exceptions aside. Administrative costs reduce the contributions going in and the amount of money put to work.

Under this analysis, the total current expenses for the plan were $75,929 or 1.31 percent a year. The total proposed expenses for the plan are $62,662 or 1.08 percent a year.

That difference—less than the price of a quality used car—each year for twenty years adds up to millions.

What is now the Great Secret may not always be.

Imagine asking an employee what he or she would rather have in twenty years:

• An envelope with a check?

• An empty envelope with a thank you note from more expensive outside financial firms that handled their money for twenty years?

Taking a Look at the RFP

The wonders of financial technology and today's computing power can provide side-by-side comparisons not even imaginable in the not-so-distant past.

One of three finalists vying for the nonprofit's contract submitted a twenty-page written proposal augmented by face-to-face interviews with the retirement investment committee. Current investment options or menu choices were compared with proposed new and continuing ones.

Sections of the analysis listed the plan's current investment choices and new selections the proposing advisor might suggest, appropriate benchmarks, the degree of diversification, respective administrative costs and tips for enhancing the plan's efficiency.

For page after page, every current choice in all asset classes was listed with performance for one, three, five and ten years. So was each suggested choice in the new proposal with past results.

Of course, there were plenty of notes along the lines of "past results may not be indicative of future performance."

By the way, this proposal was for one of the three finalists, but it did not win the contract. In the client's opinion—the opinion that matters—there was a better fit.

Summary

Fulfilling your fiduciary obligations as a plan sponsor doesn't have to mean being a full-time expert. It *can* just mean doing your due diligence to find that expert, someone with a good track record who will take the time to listen to the needs of your company—and then letting them do what they do best.

CHAPTER TWELVE

Closing the Deal in Choosing an Expert

If reading thus far has led you to the consideration that your employees may be best-served by having an outside expert, an independent fiduciary, as their investment advisor, there is one step remaining, and that is choosing the advisor.

The Day Mom Shattered My Business Plan

"How did I get into this business?" That's often the way I begin my public financial presentations. Here is what I call, "Mom's Story:"

How did I get started in this retirement finance business, a guy of thirty back then, helping people in their late sixties?

That was when I was a lot younger, a lot thinner, and with a lot more hair on my head. And the story really starts with my mother.

My mother, in this glamor-shot from the 1940s.

Mom had a hard life. She grew up in East St. Louis, Illinois, living above the family hardware store. Yes, everything you have heard about East St. Louis is true. Only worse.

East St. Louis was the site of the worst race riots in the United States in 1917. In fact, Mom's grandfather—my great-grandfather—was shot and killed in those riots.

Mom was born in 1925, the youngest of seven kids. So, her childhood was during the Great Depression. Then came Pearl Harbor and her older brothers went off to war. Mom and her father worked the hardware store. She held her own—she was a speed demon zipping down the hardware aisles.

Later she met my dad, and I was the youngest of their three kids. Mom and I always had a special relationship. My brother and sister were very jealous, but I was clearly her favorite. So there!

Dad died of a sudden heart attack at age forty-nine. Mom was a widow at forty-six, leaving her with the hardest job of all. She had to raise three teenage kids. She was grieving. She was working, struggling to keep the family together, struggling to keep the money together.

She sent all three of us off to college. I graduated from the University of Washington with a master's in business administration. My interest was taxes—not the normal kind, but the ones some call death taxes, the taxes on very large estates.

Anyone here need help on an estate of $5 million, maybe even $10, $25, $100 or $500 million? No? Okay, moving right along.

If you have an estate of that size, you become the IRS's best friend. You may owe 40 percent of your net worth to the government and the IRS wants it in cash within nine months of the death of the surviving spouse.

My specialty became helping the estate come up with the cash. That led to getting connected with the self-storage industry. Self-storage, you see, is a great business but the money is all tied up in the buildings. There is not a lot of cash.

So, I started writing an estate-planning column for the self-storage industry association. I'd get calls like, "Our buildings are worth $74 million but we only have $2 million in cash. I want to learn more about this estate tax business."

Well, one day I got a call from Mom and it went like this:

"You know, my birthday is coming up next week."

"I know Mom, I'm going to take you out for coffee and give you your present."

"I don't need your present."

"Like it or not, Mom, I'm going to give you a present."

"What I really need is for you to help me with that stuff."

"What stuff?"

"Didn't they teach you anything at that university? The 'age of sixty-five' stuff for a widow."

I should explain that Mom, a child of the Depression, was very frugal. As in, cheap. Later, after I had helped her to relocate from East St. Louis to Tucson, Arizona, I visited and saw that her house slippers had holes in them.

"Mom, let me buy you a new pair."

"No, I don't need that. You should save your money for your old age."

I knew better than to argue with my mom. So I said, "What if we go to Home Depot and buy some duct tape?"

"Well, that would be good. They are getting drafty."

I had promised to get her the "age-of-sixty-five-widow" stuff by the next Wednesday. This was before voice mail, before the internet. I started calling government offices.

Of course, you get put on hold and hear wonderful Muzak, like thirteen violins playing Rolling Stones.

A typical call to a government office, say Medicare, would go like this:

"I need to get some information for my mother about . . ."

"Sir, if your mother wants information we must talk directly to her. Goodbye."

"But . . ."

"Sorry." Click

Social Security hardly went any better.

"I would like to get your brochure on . . ."

"I'm sorry but that brochure is out of print. We expect to have more in seven to ten weeks."

Wednesday came.

"Whaddu you got?"

"Well, Mom, I called and . . ."

She gives me a look. She crosses her arms.

"You got squat, don't you? What did they teach you at that college, Mr. Fancy Pants? Now you're writing articles for rich dead people, but you can't help your own mother?"

Mom over the years.

Amid the teasing, that stung. It got my head screwed on straight. I realized I would rather help people in the here and now. It took a while to turn my business life around, but I did. And I love it.

MORAL

I was able to help my mother relocate to Tucson and to a somewhat easier life. I came to realize that living people need help with retirement preparations and that even people involved with retirement tax shelters—company owners (plan sponsors) and advisors—need help, too. Today I am a retirement advisor, helping living people in a new way—because of something Mom said.

We're in this book's final chapter on avoiding 401(k) mistakes and offering employees a better retirement program.

Along the way, we've learned the most common mistakes and just how costly they can be in terms of time and headaches in making peace with the Internal Revenue Service. Of course, it is better to do it right the first time. Unfortunately, doing it right on the first try involves keeping abreast of regulatory changes, key court rulings, and numerous IRS bulletins, and may entail more experience, training, and supervision than the typical HR department has. The solution by now should be obvious: Hire an expert.

An independent expert allows the plan sponsor, i.e., company management, to devote time to minding the business while farming out the workload and much of the responsibility.

You're not alone if you were surprised to learn just how much high fees raid from the money you thought you and fellow employees were investing, and how that can compound to very significant sums over the course of fifteen, twenty or twenty-five years.

Don't Get Mad, Get a Fiduciary

If you aren't angry about discovering that your current plan administrator may be putting his interests—not yours—first, well, you should be. The simplest way to put your interests first, without waiting for a regulatory helping hand to materialize, is to hire a credentialed fiduciary to handle your plan. As we discussed, there are many advantages to having a fiduciary on your side, in your corner, and looking out for your best interest.

In a previous chapter, we outlined how to do a request for proposals after first deciding what is most important to your company and your employees.

Perhaps you decided to do your RFP in two steps, a mailer to likely prospects to administer the retirement program and, after winnowing, face-to-face interviews between each finalist and the investment committee.

If so, it is time for some salesmanship.

First, each finalist is likely to cite the advantages that the small independent brings to the table, as opposed to a mega-brokerage firm or a national insurance company with dozens of products and a shrinking market share of 401(k) administration.

Were representatives of these giant players in the room, there might be some "... but, but, buts." They are not present, however, just independents making a pitch one at a time and an investment committee trying to decide, "Which one fits our needs best?"

So, what are the structural advantages the independents tell you they bring to the table?

• Most likely the independent advisor is a fiduciary, putting you first. Insurance agents and retail stock brokers typically are not. A sweeping regulatory change could bring wholesale personnel changes eliminating uncertified sales people and prompt corporate restructurings for mega-brokerages and insurance companies. Or not, if a regulatory revamping that has been years in the making by the Department of Labor and more recently the Securities and Exchange Commission is rolled back. Either way, credentialed independents already are fiduciaries and bring your company certainty on that score.

• Independents may hire a brokerage to be custodians of the money, handle the financial transactions and keep the records. They are not employees of the nationally branded firms and need not be influenced to choose their products, especially when they are inferior.

• Insurance companies are in the business of selling insurance—annuities. Annuities are not transparent, and the hidden cost is next to impossible to research. Group variable annuities are so opaque that it may be difficult to get answers to your questions of "What is your benchmark?" and "Did you actually beat the benchmark you selected during recent years?"

• The biggest oxymoron of choosing an insurance product is this, independents say: A 401(k) plan is a tax shelter with Uncle Sam not getting his cut until years later when money is withdrawn. An annuity is a tax-deferred vehicle. They are both tax deferred. **There is no such thing as double tax deferral.** You don't get bonus points for owning a tax-deferred product within a tax shelter. Why pay additional fees to do so?

Depending upon their personality, the finalists may be brutal or diplomatic about the stumbling giant in this David-versus-Goliath match-up.

What's next in this round of salesmanship is for the finalist to sell herself, himself or the firm.

It goes something like this:

I'm J.D. Kaiser (call me "Jay"), a 401(k) advisor and financial industry veteran based in Seattle. You selected me as a finalist. I feel we have a good fit and I want to tell you why I am the best choice to handle your account.

Here is my contact information:
J.D. Kaiser, MBA, Accredited Investment Fiduciary ®
President, 401k Rescue Experts
6023 Roosevelt Way NE
Seattle, WA 98115
(206) 362-0503
info@401kRescueExperts.com

The acronyms mean that I earned a master's degree in business administration from the University of Washington, and that I am an Accredited Investment Fiduciary® professional, earning the designation for specialized knowledge from the Center for Fiduciary Studies, and meaning I am bound by their Code of Ethics and Conduct Standards.

I began my career in estate planning and wealth preservation, later shifting to retirement planning and retirement program administration. I founded a retirement class and used a simple dot-com address to help plug people in to my educational program. My firm has since expanded with both retail and wholesale sides and more modern web addresses. The goal then—as it is now—was to offer down-to-earth guidance on retirement planning. The class was very popular, and I have a two-inch-high stack of laudatory reviews from participants. I believe that experience gives me a unique understanding of what participants, especially millennials, want in a 401(k).

I'm independent. There's no boss at, say, Merrill Lynch (or name a firm), telling me what to do and, by the way, to sell more product.

I have no preconceived advice to give you. That's why I studied your request for proposals very carefully and asked some clarifying questions to make certain I know what is important to you in a retirement program.

I don't stand alone. I help my 401(k) plan sponsors find the custodian and recordkeeper that is the best fit for their individual needs. I have some fine people and plenty of resources behind me to fill in any gaps in my knowledge and to tweak my proposal to make it an efficient blend of investment choices with low administrative fees.

The latest high-powered technology is behind me as well, through an organization called fi360. Each investment choice in your portfolio will meet twelve strict criteria that I have set. Should market conditions change or an investment vehicle falter, a replacement can be determined at computer speed. Again, according to the criteria that I believe are most appropriate for your company and employees.

Employees want education in the form of broad generic guidance. I believe I have unparalleled experience in that respect.

By now, you appreciate that you need a fiduciary who follows best practices, offers a solid educational component, uses the latest financial software to monitor performance and is supported by a national firm with great customer service.

I am the expert you are seeking.

Improving an existing 401(k) program or starting one from scratch to have tailored investment choices with low fees need not be complicated. Hiring an expert, an independent advisor, is a way to delegate the complexity: the research and knowledge, the recordkeeping and detail work, and much of the liability.

A tax-sheltered 401(k) program, efficiently managed, is a popular employee benefit that your company can offer at very little cost. Compare the company match and a modest amount of administrative overhead for the investment committee and computerized payroll with the thousands of dollars of cost in providing health insurance to an employee and dependents.

You've got a business to run. Back to what you know best.

(It's okay, Mom. I know you always taught me to be humble and you certainly knew how to cut me down to size. But you can't be humble in a job interview.)

I love what I do. It feels great to be the champion to the people I help. I want to help you be the champion for your personal financial situation, your professional career, and to be the best ally for all of your employees.

J.D. KAISER

About the Author

J.D. Kaiser, MBA, Accredited Investment Fiduciary® and President, 401(k) Rescue Experts.

J.D. Kaiser earned his Master of Business Administration degree from the University of Washington. He began his career in estate planning and wealth preservation and soon became a national expert in retirement planning. When it became clear how much money people—including his own mom—could lose due to fears, myths, and misunderstandings about retirement, he developed Retirement Class, a t-part, six-hour curriculum, to offer his own down-to-earth, "no BS" steps to retirement planning.

J.D. earned the Accredited Investment Fiduciary (AIF) designation from the Center for Fiduciary Studies. An AIF means he brings specialized knowledge of fiduciary responsibility, can implement policies and procedures that meet defined standards, and agrees to abide by the Center for Fiduciary Studies Code of Ethics and Conduct Standards. As a fiduciary, he's legally bound to work for your best interests, not his own. As he says, "It's the right thing to do, and I couldn't imagine doing it any other way."

As a business owner, an investment professional, an M.B.A., and an Accredited Investment Fiduciary®, it would be difficult to match the depth of service, experience, and insight that J.D. has to offer regarding advising on 401(k)s.

To this book's readers, J.D. extends two complimentary offers:

1) Learn how your company's plan compares in cost to what is available. Just send the name of the plan to www.401k-Score.com.
2) Want to know how the investment performance of your company's plan compares to those of similar size firms in the industry? For a benchmark, just send to www.401k-Benchmark.com. Please submit the plan statements and the 408(b)(2) disclosure.

GLOSSARY

Twenty Terms Every Plan Sponsor Must Know

Following are the twenty terms it is essential for a 401(k) plan sponsor to know. This isn't a complete list by any means—the financial industry is full of jargon and technical terms—but if you aren't somewhat familiar with the terms on this list, it may be difficult to decipher the average brochure about your 401(k) plan.

401(k) Plan. It is a defined contribution plan where an employee can make contributions from his or her paycheck either before or after tax, depending on the options offered in the plan. The contributions go into a 401(k) account, with the employee often choosing the investments based on options provided under the plan. Some employers make matching or partially matching contributions to the employee's account, up to a certain percentage. SIMPLE and safe harbor 401(k) plans have mandatory employer contributions.

403(b) Tax-Sheltered Annuity. A TSA plan is a retirement plan offered by public schools and certain tax-exempt organizations. An individual's 403(b) annuity can be obtained only under an employer's TSA plan. Generally, these annuities are funded by elective deferrals made under salary reduction agreements and non-elective employer contributions.

The Plan Document. This is a specific document required by law that governs the plan. It is a customized document specific to the company providing the 401(k) plan.

Summary plan description. It is simply The Plan Document summarized. This is available for the participants to view.

Contributions. This is the money the employee participant has deducted from the paycheck before taxes.

Matching contribution. This is money the employer puts into the participant's account. There is a specified limit. For example, a company may choose to match 4 percent of each employee's contributions up to a certain dollar limit. Employer contributions are not mandatory.

Contribution limit. Every year the IRS specifies how much money a participant can contribute in a given year. As of 2019 it is $19,000.

Catch-up contribution. If the participant is age 50 or older the annual limit is raised to $26,000 as of 2019.

Mutual funds. Mutual funds are investments that pool your money together with other investors to purchase shares of a collection of stocks, bonds or other securities, referred to as a portfolio, that might be difficult to re-create on your own. Mutual funds are typically overseen by a portfolio manager.

Exchange-traded funds (ETFs). An exchange-traded fund (ETF) is a basket of securities you buy or sell through a brokerage firm on a stock exchange. ETFs are offered on virtually all asset classes ranging from traditional investments to alternative assets like commodities or currencies. ETFs can be traded like stocks—at any time of the day—and usually designed to mirror an index. ETFs generally have lower fees than mutual funds.

Expense ratio. The expense ratio is the annual fee that all mutual funds or ETFs charge their shareholders. It expresses the percentage of assets deducted each fiscal year for fund expenses, including 12b-1 fees, management fees, administrative fees, operating costs, and all other asset-based costs incurred by the funds.

Not included in the expense ratio are other expenses for mutual funds or ETFs. Portfolio transaction fees, or brokerage costs, as well as initial or deferred sales charges are examples. The expense ratio, which is deducted from the fund's net assets, is accrued on a daily basis.

Other expenses for mutual funds. There are many. Forbes did an entire article on hidden fees. See "How Much Do Mutual Funds Really Cost?" by Kenneth Kim.[15]

Other expenses in ETFs. Tom Lydon's "ETF of the Week" for MarketWatch show pointed out that ETFs impose fees for costs incurred when changes are made in the underlying index. These costs are not disclosed.[16]

Index. The composite figure for a group of stocks, bonds, or commodities as in the thirty-stock Dow Jones Industrial Average. An index often serves as the performance benchmark for an actively traded mutual fund.

Revenue-sharing fees. Mutual funds offer to share part of their fees with advisors who bring them business. This creates unfairness as some plan participants pay a larger portion of mutual fund administrative costs than participants who escape these fees.

Broker. A broker earns a commission on products sold and does not have to act in the client's best interest. The broker only has to show that the product is suitable for the client.

---

[15] Kenneth Kim. Forbes. Sept. 24, 2016, "How Much Do Mutual Funds Really Cost?" https://www.forbes.com/sites/kennethkim/2016/09/24/how-much-do-mutual-funds-really-cost/#5c22825ea527

[16] Tom Lydon, Market Watch. "ETF of the Week." June 30, 2016. Podcast: https://www.etftrends.com/2016/06/podcast-a-better-way-to-play-ETF-mid-caps/

Fiduciary. A fiduciary charges a management fee and has to act in the client's best interest. Advisors known as 3-21 fiduciaries select funds out of a larger group for a company plan but leave the final decision to the plan sponsor (company owner). Advisors known as 3-38 fiduciaries also make the final decision. The 3-38 fiduciaries remove much liability from the plan sponsor.

In-service distribution. These are withdrawals before an individual reaches a triggering event such as attaining age fifty-nine-and-one-half or leaving employ. Some plans allow for early withdrawals (in-service distributions) to make house payments or pay for children's education. These withdrawals often carry a 10 percent tax penalty.

The magic of fifty-nine-and-a-half. Individuals in tax-sheltered retirement accounts reaching this age can withdraw their money without tax penalties.

Pension. Traditional pensions, also known as defined-benefit plans, are on their way out. They commit the employer to paying definite amounts in retirement under formulas based on the employee's salary, length of service, and age at retirement. Employees can draw those benefits either as one-time lump-sum payments or monthly annuities for their lifetime (and if elected, the lifetime of a spouse).

STANDARDS

Accredited Investment Fiduciary® Standards

To my clients, I will:[17]

1. Employ and provide the client information on the Prudent Practices when serving as an investment fiduciary and/or advising other investment fiduciaries.
2. Act with honesty and integrity and avoid conflicts of interest, real or perceived.
3. Ensure the timely and understandable disclosure of relevant information that is accurate, complete, and objective.
4. Be responsible when determining the value of my services and my form of compensation; taking into consideration the time, skill, experience, and special circumstances involved in providing my services.

---

[17] Fi360, Inc. 2016. "Code of Ethics."
https://fi360.zendesk.com/hc/en-us/articles/203684238-Code-of-Ethics.

5. Know the limits of my expertise and refer my clients to colleagues and/or other professionals in connection with issues beyond my knowledge and skills.
6. Respect the confidentiality of information acquired in the course of my work, and not disclose such information to others, except when authorized or otherwise legally obligated to do so. I will not use confidential information acquired in the course of my work for my personal advantage.
7. Not exploit any relationship or responsibility that has been entrusted to me.

To my community, I will:
1. Proactively promote and be a steward of ethical behavior as a responsible partner among my peers in the work environment and in my community.
2. Ensure that the overall promotion of my practice is implemented in the best interests of my profession.
3. Seek, accept, and offer honest criticism of technical work; acknowledge and correct errors; and properly credit the contributions of others.
4. Use corporate assets and resources employed or entrusted to me in a responsible manner.
5. Continue to improve my knowledge and skills, share ideas and information with colleagues, and assist them in their professional development.

Who Is a Fiduciary?[18]

Fi360 defines an investment fiduciary as someone who is providing investment advice or managing the assets of another person and stands in a special relationship of trust, confidence and/or legal responsibility.

Investment fiduciaries can be divided generally into three groups: Investment Stewards, Investment Advisors, and Investment Managers.

An Investment Steward is a person who has the legal responsibility for managing investment decisions, including plan sponsors, trustees and investment committee members.

An Investment Advisor is a professional who is responsible for providing investment advice and/or managing investment decisions. Investment Advisors include wealth managers, financial advisors, trust officers, financial consultants, investment consultants, financial planners and fiduciary advisers.

An Investment Manager is a professional who has discretion to select specific securities for separate accounts, mutual and exchange-traded funds, commingled trusts and unit trusts.

---

[18] Fi360, Inc. 2016. "Prudent Practices."
https://www.fi360.com/resources/prudent-practices

www.ingramcontent.com/pod-product-compliance
Lightning Source LLC
Chambersburg PA
CBHW070640220526
45466CB00001B/242